NO PLACE LIKE HOME

1830 1890

no place like home

*A History of Domestic Architecture
in Springfield & Clark County, Ohio*

by George H. Berkhofer

George H. Berkhofer

ORANGE FRAZER PRESS
Wilmington, Ohio

ISBN-978-1-933197-25-8

Copyright © 2007 The Harry M. and Violet Turner Charitable Trust

No part of this publication may be reproduced in any material form (including photocopying or storing in any medium by electronic means and whether or not transiently or incidentally to some other use of this publication) without the written permission of the copyright holder except in accordance with the provisions of the Copyright, Designs and Patents Act 1988.

Published for The Turner Foundation by:
Orange Frazer Press
P.O. Box 214, Wilmington, OH 45177
Telephone 1.800.852.9332 for price and shipping information.
www.orangefrazer.com

The Turner Foundation
4 West Main Street
Suite 800
Springfield, Ohio 45502
www.hmturnerfoundation.org
937.325.1300

art direction John Baskin & Jeff Fulwiler
interior design John Baskin with assistance from Chad DeBoard
project coordinator for The Turner Foundation Tamara K. Dallenbach
technical assistance Chad DeBoard & Tim Fauley
cover design Jeff Fulwiler
cover photograph Roderick J. Hatfield

Library of Congress Cataloging-in-Publication Data

Berkhofer, George H.
  No place like home : a history of domestic architecture in Springfield and Clark County, Ohio / by George H. Berkhofer.
    p. cm.
  Includes bibliographical references and index.
  ISBN 978-1-933197-25-8
  1. Architecture, Domestic--Ohio--Springfield. 2. Architecture, Domestic--Ohio--Clark County. 3. Springfield (Ohio)--Buildings, structures, etc. I. Title.
  NA7238.S67B47 2007
  728.09771'49--dc22

                                          2006039610

Printed in Canada

Dedication

I dedicate this book to my dear wife, Karen.
I consider it the greatest compliment of all that she has enjoyed what I have written,
and I hope those who read this book will be as fortunate in their choice of spouse as I.

no place like home

Acknowledgements

Perhaps the most difficult task for any author is to compile a list of those to whom thanks are owed. The ever present worry is that someone will be forgotten, or another will be slighted. The following, then, is the best that my poor memory can produce.

In any such listing, of course, family must come first. I can never adequately express my gratitude to Karen, my wife of thirty-seven years, as well as my children, Elizabeth, Julia and George. It was the support and confidence of my wife during the initial composition in the 1970s and that of the entire family in more recent days, who suggested to me that I could complete this project. None of this would have happened without them.

Had it not been for everyone involved in the original *A New Concept* magazine, little of this would ever have seen the light of day. Although their day is long past, I still owe them the greatest of thanks. Yet, after the initial interest had died, all of this information lay dormant, like the grave goods in a pharaoh's tomb, just awaiting discovery.

The trail from tomb to daylight has been filled with good people and fine adventures. This began in the spring of 2005 when I received the first annual Springfield Preservation Alliance's Spirit of Preservation Award. This was given for work in earlier days, especially for the fifteen articles which became this book. I am especially grateful to Tamara Dallenbach and Kevin Rose for their confidence in me and the award.

In a manner of speaking, I am also grateful to my former employers in my last position. By late summer in 2005, they had decided they no longer needed my services as a technician to help run their business. Without this impetus, I might still be their clerk.

I can never give enough thanks to Anne Benston, whom I have known for most of my professional life. Her many years of loyal friendship and good offices are purely a wonder to me. Without her I have no idea what I might be doing today. It was through Anne that Tamara and Kevin became interested in the idea of my becoming associated with The Turner Foundation.

Without this Foundation and its magnificent commitment to preserving the rich heritage of local history, there is little possibility that this work would ever have been resurrected. Of course, the organization consists of not only resources, but even more important, people. Everyone, from the executive director, John Landess, down, has shown me the greatest courtesy and every assistance. It is simply impossible to say enough good things about these people.

Few people have been more patient and hard-working in this project than Virginia Weygandt and Kasey Eichensehr of the Clark County Historical Society. They have spent countless hours researching and scanning the illustrations for this book, and they have my deepest gratitude.

At the same time, I must thank Emily Rottenborn of The Turner Foundation for her outstanding computer work. It was Emily who patiently processed almost daily changes in the illustrations. Miraculously, she managed to keep everything in far better order than did I.

Springfield, Ohio
2007

Chapters

Introduction / page xiii

Chapter one / page two
Homes of the first generation

Chapter two / page eight
Houses—log or stone?

Chapter three / page sixteen
Working with bricks

Chapter four / page twenty-six
Athens on Buck Creek?

Chapter five / page thirty-six
Rise and fall of a Greek empire

Chapter six / page forty-six
Getting to the point

Chapter seven / page sixty-four
Italian intermezzo

Chapter eight / page seventy-six
Garbled Italian

Chapter nine / page eighty-four
More garbled Italian

Chapter ten / page ninety-four
French curves

Chapter eleven / page one hundred twelve
Olde English

Chapter twelve / page one hundred twenty-four
What's in a name?

Chapter thirteen / page one hundred forty-two
turn backward, turn backward

Chapter fourteen / page one hundred fifty-six
pares cum paribus congregantur

Chapter fifteen / page one hundred seventy
a few more encores

Chapter sixteen / page one hundred eighty
and still more encores

Bibliography / page one hundred ninety-seven

Sources of images / page one hundred ninety-nine

Index / page two hundred and three

Introduction

The volume you have before you originated in 1976 as a contribution to the Bicentennial Celebration of the American Revolution. It was a small pamphlet, but the text and images quickly found favor with the public and the author was soon asked to teach a course in local architectural history for Clark State Community College.

During the winter of 1976-1977, a monthly magazine was established in Springfield with the name *A New Concept*. The author, who was then Executive Director of the Clark County Historical Society, was asked to be a contributing editor for an architectural series. The group of articles, like the original pamphlet, was well received by the public and was continued for fifteen issues. Following the architectural series, the author wrote another one on the history of local photography. This latter ended incomplete when the magazine foundered in 1979.

Although the author was asked on several occasions to repeat the course, the magazine text gradually became an obscure, if not literally, lost artifact. By the year 2005, there were only three known sets of the magazine: one was held by the Clark County Historical Society, one by the Clark County Public Library, and one by the author.

Recognizing and examining this situation with a critical eye, The Turner Foundation felt that the magazine texts should be updated and joined together. The ensuing book is not one of those "Lost …" books in which the reader is asked to attend, as it were, a tearful architectural wake or funeral. On the contrary, this book was published with a hope. The hope is that it will stir the minds and imaginations of Springfielders to love, cherish, and preserve what has heretofore survived from the past.

NO PLACE LIKE HOME

Primne
HOMES OF THE FI

When the English language took the French word *pionnier* and converted it into pioneer, it was used to describe a class of soldiers whose duty it was to precede an army and remove any obstructions from the route of march. It would be difficult to determine who first applied that term to a civilian who penetrated a wilderness, cleared the land, built a home and sowed crops. Yet, whoever that person was, he could not have chosen a more apt word to describe such an individual.

The pioneer did not just clear the road of obstructions, but rather actually created the first roads, or "traces," in the primeval forests. For him the woods were the obstructions thrown up by the enemy, Nature. His home had to be built by removing the obstructive trees and his fields were prepared in the same way. Like the soldier who was enrolled as a pioneer, the civilian, too, was clearing the way for an army. That army was the mass of restless people who would move to a new territory when they had finally abandoned hope of a satisfying or rewarding life in settled areas. This thumbnail sketch is as true of Clark County as anywhere else in Ohio.

Although the debate as to who was the first settler in Clark County and when he arrived has lasted for more than a century, it is clear that a trickle of settlers was arriving by various routes in the late 1790s. Once arrived, the first necessity was to provide some sort of shelter from the weather.

A quick glance at the early topographical maps made of the area between 1802 and 1805 shows that most parts of the county were forested, to one degree or another. Nature, the enemy, had thrown up an obstacle; yet, in doing so, it had provided the ready material with which the pioneer might construct the very shelter he needed so desperately. Out of necessity came the genesis of the log cabin.

1 (above). View of a dugout, or "subterranean" house at Plimoth Plantation, Plymouth, Massachusetts.
2 (at left). Woodcut of a dugout log hut, entitled, "The Clearing," Ladies Repository Magazine, 1855.
3 (below). A 1930s photograph of the supposed site of a dugout hut on the Simon Kenton Farm.

FIRST GENERATION

chapter ONE

8 Drawing, "Dalzell's Clearing Near Piqua, Ohio", by Thomas Wharton, 1831.

The original log cabin had virtually nothing in common with those structures nowadays described as such, and for which plans or blueprints are often advertised in magazines. In fact, the first type of log cabin was not even the sort of building depicted in later nineteenth-century woodcuts and engravings. Although photography was invented too late to record the Ohio log cabin in its earliest form, it is clear that they were close to the "subterranean" house concept of Plimoth Plantation in New England, and the "dugout" shelters of early Kansas *(fig. 1, page 3)*.

These homes were created by first digging a shallow excavation in the ground. Then logs were fitted together to create the upper part of the walls. Finally, brushwood and saplings were cut and more or less woven together to form a roof. A temporary home of this type is shown in an old engraving in Figure 2 *(page 2)*. Figure 3 *(page 3)* shows a depression in the ground at the Simon Kenton Farm on U.S. 68 North, across from the Navistar plant, where Kenton *(fig. 4, page 6)*, is supposed to have created his first shelter. Homes of this kind were highly perishable and transitory at best. As soon as the pioneer had the leisure, he began to build a somewhat more permanent home and thus entered Phase Two of the log cabin.

The second phase of log construction brings us much closer to the classical form of cabin familiar to the modern mind. Its origins, however, are obscure. Some have traced it to a building technique imported into Delaware by early Swedish settlers; others attribute it to German immigrants, and still others to Native American prototypes. Whatever the source, it is certain that it is not English in origin. The earliest English settlers built, insofar as they were able, along the lines of half-timbered, framed and thatched homes which they knew in the Mother Country *(fig. 5, page 7)*.

The kind of log building *(fig. 6, page 7)*, we are now discussing was, contrary to

page 5

*4 (above). An 1860s woodcut portrait of Simon Kenton.
9 (background screen). Woodcut, "The Raising," ca. 1830, from The Western Miscellany.*

popular belief, never intended to be permanent. In most cases, the pioneer expected to live in it for a few years until he had accumulated enough wealth to build a more substantial home. In some cases the expectation was fulfilled; after a few years a new brick or frame house was built and the old cabin razed. In other cases, where fortune did not come to the owner, the house was used until he moved or died, and then allowed to fall into decay and ruins. As a result of this attitude, virtually all of the examples of this phase of log construction have utterly disappeared, surviving only in nineteenth-century woodcuts, sketches or engravings.

These houses were of relatively simple construction. They consisted of one or two ground-floor rooms with walls of logs, which had been notched to interlock and fit together. A fireplace was built at one end. The firebox was again made of notched logs and the chimney of small, trimmed branches. The inside of both was smeared with mud to provide fire resistance.

The gaps between the wall logs were "chinked," or filled with mud and other readily available debris. Most of this material consisted of wooden chips and slices removed from the logs by adzing, in the process of notching or squaring them for construction. In later examples, a kind of lime mortar was used with the rubble for chinking.

The roof was covered with "shakes," or thin slabs split off from a log with a hand tool called a froe. This roofing of shakes was usually held in place by a series of long poles running across the shakes, with the poles themselves being fastened to the rafters underneath by wooden pins. Sometimes rocks were laid on the shakes, resting against the poles, for added security. Adults usually slept in the ground-floor rooms, and the children in the loft under the roof. The children often awakened on winter mornings with a layer of snow on their bedclothes due to this insecure roofing technique.

Figure 7 *(at far right)* shows a log cabin that was constructed in 1901 by the Springfield Centennial Committee. While there are a few technical errors, it does give a good idea of the appearance of a log cabin built in this Second Phase style. It was later moved to the 400 block of East High Street and modern material replaced the shake roof.

In 1831, an amateur British artist, Thomas Wharton, visited the new Springfield settler, Jeremiah Warder. Wharton and Warder had made each other's acquaintance when Warder, as a young man, had toured England. Now Wharton was on a tour of the United States, and made numerous sketches in the area. Although Figure 8 *(previous page)* was done near Piqua, it is equally representative of the Springfield area. It shows a typical pioneer's clearing. In the foreground is his field with charred trees and stumps, around which he farmed. In the distance is his cabin with all of the classic features perfectly visible.

It is perhaps needless to remark that not every newcomer to Clark County followed the two-step pattern of log cabin construction. Many a settler, who arrived in an area where there were neighbors, was able, with their help ❋ *(fig. 9, background screen at left)* to build immediately a cabin of the second style, bypassing the crude first style. Other early arrivals with specialized skills often built in completely different forms, such as brick or stone. This occurred most often in villages where others with varied building skills could be found. However, *Dalzell's Clearing Near Piqua (pages 4 & 5)* is probably a view typical of the Clark County countryside and its homes, up to the 1830s.

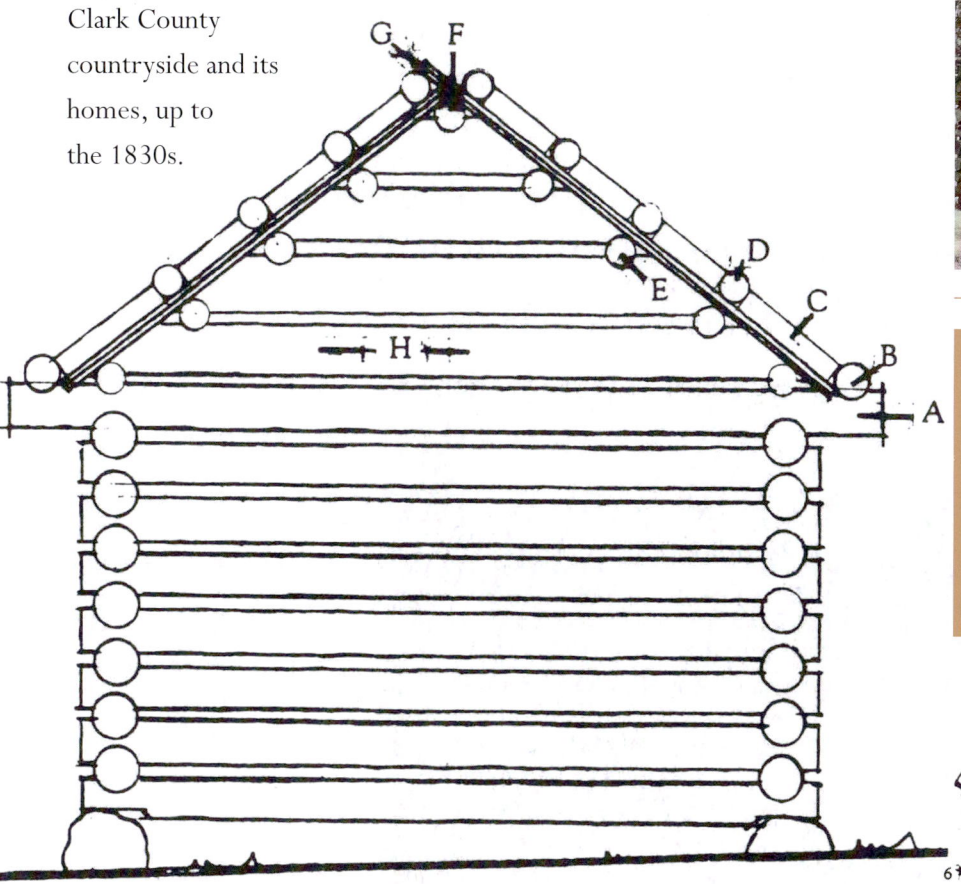

5 *(above). Re-creation of a typical, English style house in Plimoth Plantation. 6 (below and left). Drawing of a typical early log cabin and its components. 7 (immediately above). Photograph of the Centennial Log Cabin, Springfield, Ohio, 1901.*

Parts of a log house.
A) Eave beam   E) Rib
B) Butting pole   F) Ridgepole
C) Knee   G) Clapboards
D) Weight pole   H) Trapping

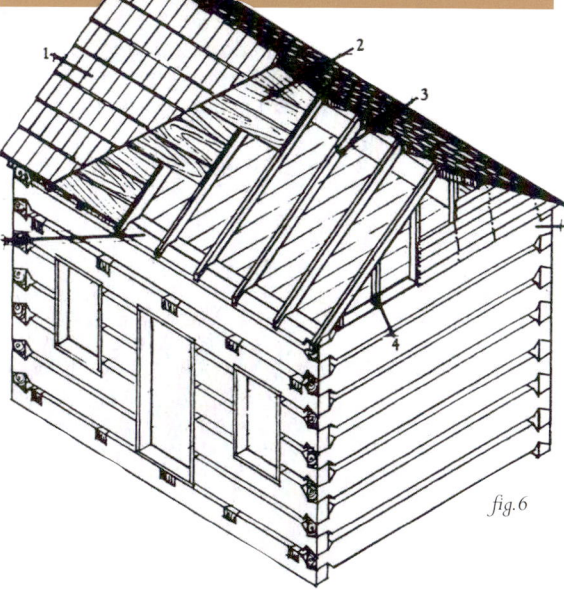

Parts of a log house.
1) Shakes or shingles   4) Stud
2) Sheathing   5) Tie beam or end girt
3) Rafter   6) Plate

Hewn
HOUSES — LOG

It is often the case that what begins as a necessity, in time becomes crystallized into standard form. Whether that form has a greater practical or aesthetic form than another may be completely immaterial. What does matter is that the form has become traditional and continues to be used for that reason. Such was the case with the Third Phase of log architecture, the log house.

Although there were numerous saw mills in Ohio by 1800, and planning mills after 1820, hand worked log architecture continued in common use up to the 1850s. Here we are not dealing with the crude huts and cabins of the first pioneers, but rather with actual houses. These were structures employing many of the standard design features of the domestic architecture of the period, with certain technical adaptations. The principal characteristic of these houses was that the exterior walls continued to be built of solid, hewn logs—not smaller, sawn timbers which had been mortised together and then pinned with wooden pegs, or nailed. These logs were usually 8" thick and, in the period 1800–1825, up to 24" wide. After 1825 the size was usually 8"x12". The ends of the logs were notched in any of several different patterns, so as to interlock with those of a cross wall ❋ *(fig. 10, at right)*.

As was the case with the cabin, the spaces between large logs were carefully filled with small debris and then covered with a sort of plaster cement—the "chinking and daubing process." Now, however, the interior of the house was very carefully finished. Lath and plaster were added to the walls, as well as neatly

10 (above). Two of the most common patterns of log notching. 11 (background screen). Wooden siding with holes for wooden pins. 12 (at left). The South Charleston Log House. 21 (below). The Jacob Huffman House, ca. 1827, Lower Valley Pike.

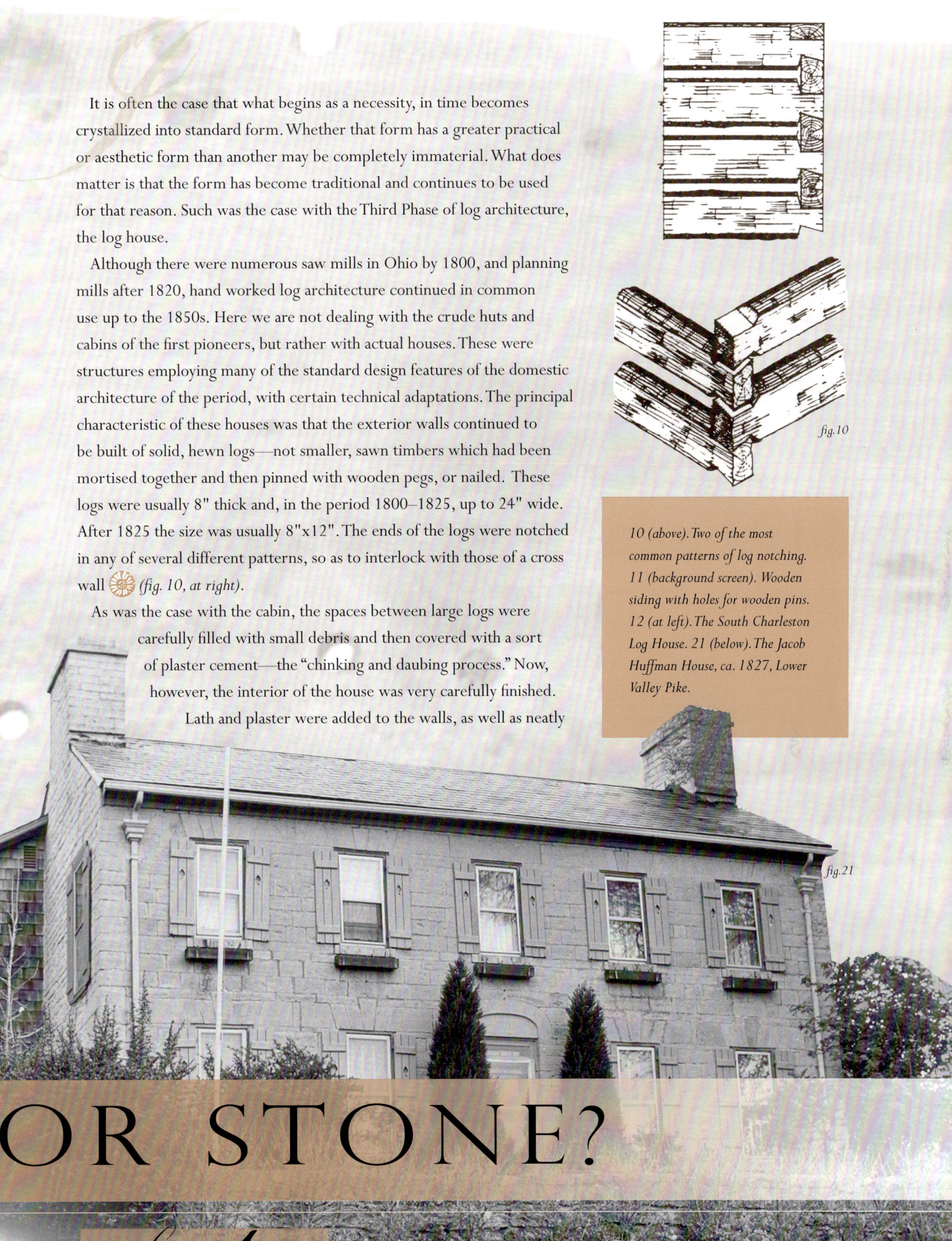

OR STONE?

hapter TWO

fig. 13

13 (above). *Board with wooden pin, from the South Charleston Log House. Note the adze markings on the edge of the board.* 14 (below). *Photograph of interior wall of the South Charleston Log House when disassembled, showing original opening for cooking fireplace.* 18 (at right). *View of exterior logs of the South Charleston Log House, showing the erosion of the ends and sides of the logs.*

fig. 14

finished woodwork in the form of mantels, chair rails, cupboards and interior plank dividing walls.

The exterior of the homes was likewise carefully finished. The surfaces of the logs were relatively smooth from the adzing process and the crevices were neatly filled with the chinking and plaster. Contrary to a romantic, popular belief, few log houses were left in a natural state with exposed logs. Those that were had a coat of lime whitewash applied, at least to the front side. Many log houses were now built specifically to have siding placed on them, and older houses routinely had it added. Some of the early siding was held in place with wooden pins, as were door and window frames, when nails were expensive or not obtainable ❋ *(fig. 11, background, previous page)*.

The South Charleston Log House ❋ *(fig. 12, previous page)*, to judge from its notching, which is "steeple," or "saddle," and its weathered log ends, dates to the period 1820–1830. It was probably built near the early center of the village at what is now the intersection of Ohio Route 41 and U.S. 42.

The house was disassembled and moved to lot 12 in the Paist and Moore addition in 1870. In the 1990s the owners gave the house to the Heritage Commission of South Charleston, with the proviso that it be removed from the lot. Once again it was taken apart and then reassembled one block away on the grounds of the Heritage Commission Depot.

When first rebuilt in 1870, the original front side was turned to the back, a new door was cut and, beside it, a long, Victorian window was created. In the 1990s reconstruction, the window was shifted to the right and shortened, to make it align with the one original window. A third window had been cut in the remaining blank side. This, too, was shortened to the dimensions of the original window. During disassembly, one board with wooden pins was recovered from the original doorway and one board with holes for pins from the original window frame ❋ *(fig. 13, left, top)*.

As the interior lath and plaster were removed during the disassembly, the gap in the wall for the great cooking fireplace was laid open to view ❋ *(fig. 14, left, bottom)*. This fireplace had been eliminated after the 1870 move as most people were cooking on iron kitchen ranges by that time. Traces of interior whitewashing also became apparent during the plaster removal.

The former Robert Brewer Log House ❋ *(fig. 15, page 13, inset)*, located on Old Springfield Road just northeast of the village of Pitchin[1], is typical of thousands that once dotted Clark County. The majority of these have vanished and most of those remaining lie hidden under modern siding.

[1] *A private individual has since acquired this house, disassembled it and moved it to another site.*

While the Brewer House has now had all of its weatherboarding removed, most log houses of its era (ca. 1830) would have presented an exterior not unlike any simple frame structure with siding *(fig. 16, next page)*.

Occasionally a log house was never sided, paint supplying the only protection to the logs. Such was the case with the Thrasher House *(fig. 17, page 15)*. This picture of the house, located in the vicinity of Thrasher St., appeared in the 1894 Clark County, Ohio, atlas. It demonstrates that even at that late date logs were sometimes still visible and well whitewashed. The whitewash, incidentally, was in the form of thin, watery, lime-based paint. In the case of the Brewer House, the lack of whitewash and the extreme sharpness of

18 *Exterior of the South Charleston Log House.*

1830

the notching, even today, indicate an early siding effort. It had not long been exposed to the weather, if at all. The South Charleston Log House, however, with its eroded log ends ✺ *(fig. 18, previous page)* shows just the opposite. It had been exposed to the weather for many years without siding. This situation may have lasted as long as until 1870 when it was moved for the first time.

While the pioneer was virtually compelled to accept and utilize log construction as his only option, the settlers who followed them, as well as the pioneers who stayed, were soon able to make choices, whether dictated by taste, money or earlier associations. The needful thing was for the settlement of new people with a background in the necessary building trades and skills.

The all-pervading style of architecture common in Clark County and other frontier areas up to 1830 is that called "Late Federal." It is rarely found in a pure form as practiced in the major cities by professional house builders. Rather, it is combined with certain local adaptations/variations, and the term *vernacular* is often added to the name. In its pure form, the Late Federal style originated in the eastern part of the country out of previous Neoclassical forms. The style was brought to Ohio chiefly by Scottish-Irish who affected the design considerably with traces of their homeland architecture. The result was a rectangular two-story house with a gable roof, usually a chimney at each gable end, and a façade that could be balanced or unbalanced. If balanced, the door was centrally placed with one or two windows on each side. If unbalanced, the door was to one side of the façade with two windows beside it and three windows across the second floor ✺ *(fig. 19, next page)*. These houses usually had a one-story wing housing the kitchen facilities. This was attached either in line with the rest of the structure, or else perpendicular to it and on the back side.

The overall effect of the Late Federal Vernacular was much like the traditional, rural architecture of a well-to-do Scottish farm. The Brewer House, like almost

16 *A simple frame house in Springfield, built about 1850, in the same style as the older log houses.*

15 *The Robert Brewer Log House, siding removed.*

every other log house, was but a very simple form of this vernacular mode. The earliest alternative construction utilizing the Late Federal Vernacular style also happens to be the earliest documented house in Clark County,[2] the Donnel House (fig. 20, bottom right).

JONATHAN DONNEL first came to this area in 1795 while working as a surveyor for Peyton Short, brother-in-law of John Cleve Symmes, the great visionary of early Ohio land speculation. Through his job as surveyor he was able to acquire the exact tract of land he wanted and built up considerable holdings over the next fifteen years.

Donnel appears to have lived in log structures at first, just like other pioneers. But, in or by 1811, he built a fine new home on a tract he owned in Section 21 of Springfield Township, near Mad River. Donnel broke with the tradition of log architecture by building his house out of limestone quarried from the cliffs of his own property. In one sense he stayed with tradition, since stone was the usual building material of the Scottish-Irish in Scotland. On the other hand, the internal, structural timbering and finish woodwork was what was being used in the better class of log houses ten to twenty years later.

Technically, then, the house was considerably in advance of its neighbors. The windows were built with carefully laid flat stone arches and the corners of the house even had specially dressed stone *quoins* emplaced for added strength. Donnel, unfortunately, did not live to enjoy his house, for he committed suicide the following spring, in April of 1812. The reasons for the suicide have never been adequately established.

The Donnel House is then a mute witness to the fact that the settler need not just accept log architecture, if he had the means or taste for something else. It was possible to build in another medium and it was apparently possible to find skilled workmen to execute the job. Stone construction, no doubt, was beyond the means of many people. It was also slow and, if not done carefully, produced a perpetually damp and chilly home. Log houses lacked these problems, but had others, such as shrinkage of the logs and rot. Brick construction was the ideal mean between the two, but was traditionally the last to appear.

The tradition begun by Jonathan Donnel of building homes out of the limestone which lines the cliffs along Buck Creek and Mad River was, regrettably, a short-lived one. As a stone emplaced at the eaves indicates, Donnel completed his house in 1811. About five years later, Gen. Benjamin Whiteman, who would have the Clark County line adjusted to exclude *his* property, constructed a stone house next to his log house near Clifton.

[2] *By the phrase "earliest documented house" is meant that there is every possibility of pre-1811 houses existing in Clark County, but whose age or existence have yet to be established. Then, too, many early homes have been remodeled beyond recognition, only adding to the research task.*

Apparently the second and last of the early stone houses in Clark County was completed about 1827 by Jacob Huffman.

Jacob Huffman and his wife, Catherine, had been immigrants from Pennsylvania, settling land in Sections 21 and 27 of Bethel Township. The house he built (fig. 21, page 9), which some say took five years to build, was erected in Section 27. The stone was cut from nearby cliffs, only a few hundred yards from the site. The structure is similar to the Donnel House in overall impact, but it is on a much larger scale. Then, too, there are certain subtle details that set it off from the Donnel, although both are in the Late Federal style[3].

The principal difference lies in the treatment of the main doorway. Whereas the Donnel has a flat arch of plain stones, the Huffman has a carved, semicircular stone *lunette* panel inserted over the door. The lunette is a simple substitution for the more elegant "fanlight" that was being used in many eastern homes. In addition, while both houses have flat stone arches over the windows, those in the Huffman House are done with a prominent central keystone in the true Federal style. Then, too, the stones comprising the walls of the Huffman are larger and more carefully dressed. Yet the pattern of laying the stone is similar and they have like cap designs to the chimneys. The Huffman, however, is a balanced design, whereas the Donnel has an off-center façade. In sum, the Huffman House is a fitting climax to the Late Federal Vernacular style of architecture as expressed in stone.

[3] There are at least three other stone houses in the county, but they belong to the 1840s, or later, and not the early innovative period.

17 (above). Photograph taken in 1894, the John Thrasher Log House in Springfield, Ohio.
19 (background screen, at left). Drawing of Federal style house, by Asher Benjamin, The American Builder's Companion, 1827.
20 (below). 1940s photograph of the Jonathan Donnel House, now fallen into rubble.

20 *Photograph taken in the 1940s of the Jonathan Donnel House.*

page 15

WORKING WITH

As we have noted before, stone construction, while giving great permanence, involved a number of difficulties, not the least of which was expense. Stone was time consuming to cut and dress, which had to be done by a trained person, and expensive to haul any great distance. Then, too, if certain rules were not followed in construction, the house would be perpetually chilly and damp. On the other hand, the difficulties of maintenance of a log house, especially the swelling and shrinking of the logs, thereby loosening the chinking, were obvious. The only alternative was brick construction.

The use of brick in house construction locally seems to have been a relatively late arrival, coming just about the same time as, or shortly after, stone. Although the initial mixing of the clay (which abounds in the area) and the shaping of the bricks is relatively easy, it would require considerable expertise to know how to build a kiln and fire the "green" bricks. The lack of someone with this knowledge may account for its lateness of introduction. An 1810 census of Cincinnati revealed the existence of 232 frame homes and 55 of log, but only 37 of brick and 14 of stone. Even in one of the large towns of Ohio, the proportion of brick and stone structures was small in the early days.

23 (at left). Scottish-Irish design transplanted to America; birthplace of Andrew Jackson, Mecklenburg County, North Carolina.
25 (below). The Estle Homestead, North River Road.

BRICKS

chapter THREE

24a Volunteers assembled at the Crabill House for the first day of reclamation work in 1973. The author is standing second from the left.

In 1881 the Beers Company's *History of Clark County, Ohio*, considered the subject of who built the first brick house in Springfield—and when—an interesting if trivial point. It reported the story that John Ambler had helped one William Ross burn brick for his own and Ross' houses in 1815. Ross built his house at Main and Market (now Fountain Avenue), while Ambler built out farther west on Main Street. Ross' house was razed in 1869, but Ambler's stood until the late 1960s. At about the same time, Maddox Fisher built a one-story house of brick adjacent to the Public Square, where the U.S. Post Office now stands. Later, in Moorefield Township, Beers reports that Alexander McBeth built the first brick house out in the county, on his property there. No matter what the specifics of the matter are, it is clear that the period 1810–1815 saw the large-scale introduction of brick construction into Clark County home building.

Of the early brick homes in the county, a quick assessment of those that are easily seen allows us to group them, albeit somewhat arbitrarily, into three bodies. The first of these, and perhaps the oldest, are those with a gable roof and a fairly massive chimney at each end. The second are those which also have a gable roof, but each end has two separate chimneys which rise straight up. The chimneys are connected by brickwork to the gable and thus, when viewed from the end, give a square outline with only two short sections rising above the masonry. The third is a subdivision of the second and consists of those houses which have two chimneys at each end, but which are not connected by brickwork.

It is tempting to classify these houses not only by the chimney designs, but also by the place of origin of the person for whom they were built. Doing it this way, one would categorize the first group as "Virginia" style and the other two as "Pennsylvania." In some cases, however, there are crossovers, such as the Huffman which is Virginia style, but built by a Pennsylvanian. It therefore seems better to assume that it was the builder who impressed the house with its major characteristics, and the actual owner opting for smaller details and decorations.

The first group, or "Virginia" style, are those houses of Scottish-Irish heritage. The basic style and all of its variants, prevail through the lowlands of Scotland, as well as northern England and Wales *(fig. 22, next page, background)*. Brought to America by immigrants in the seventeenth and eighteenth centuries, it quickly became the prevailing building style in Virginia, as well as creeping into adjacent areas such as Pennsylvania and Kentucky after the Revolutionary War.

28 J. C. Fuller House, Ohio 41 & New Carlisle-St. Paris Pike, built ca. 1846.

24b The David Crabill House, grounds of the C. J. Brown Reservoir, built ca. 1826.

26 The "Dr. Nehls" House, Rt. 41 & U.S. Rt. 42, South Charleston, Ohio, built ca. 1830.

These were houses of usually two stories with a gable roof. A massive chimney at each end served the fireplaces on both floors. A kitchen wing was built either in line with, or perpendicular to, the main body of the house. In Clark County such homes had either two or four rooms down and the like number upstairs. Due to the complexities of fireplace flue construction, two rooms down and up was the norm. Up until the late eighteenth century, the fireboxes and chimneys were built on the outside of the house walls (fig. 23, page 16). After about 1780, and the experiments in heat efficiency conducted by Sir Benjamin Thompson, Count Rumford, the chimneys began to be moved inside the house walls to conserve heat. Cabins and poorer homes continued to use the outside chimney up to the Civil War.

The interiors of such structures were relatively plain. The walls were plastered and painted white, sometimes with applied stenciling. A painted chair rail of decorative, wooden molding was attached to the walls of most rooms, about three feet above the floor. This prevented the backs of chairs from rubbing and disfiguring the walls. Depending on the wealth of the family, the fireplace mantels could be the most elegant pieces of woodwork in the house. After 1800 they were usually done in the current Neoclassical designs popular in the East, and painted. A wooden cupboard, likewise painted, was usually built between the fireplace and the outside wall. These cupboards were used to hold anything, from china to clothes, depending on the use of the room. Stairways could also be either very utilitarian or highly finished, with turned balusters, newel posts and wooden cutouts applied to the ends of the steps.

Some of the well-known examples of this style of brick building in Clark County are: The David Crabill House, 1826, above the C. J. Brown Reservoir (fig's. 24a, page 18; 24b, left); the Estle Homestead on North River Road (fig. 25, page 17); the Dr. Nehls House, ca. 1830, in South Charleston at Rts. 41 & U.S. 42 (fig. 26, left)); the Buena Vista Tavern, 1835, U.S. 40 at Buena Vista Road (fig. 27, top, right); and the J. C. Fuller House, Ohio 41 and New Carlisle-St. Paris Pike (fig. 28, left).

What we have called the "Pennsylvania" style and its variants has a long and complex history. It may have evolved out of the British custom, especially in the eighteenth century, of building long rows of houses with party walls in their towns. The term "party wall" refers to a construction technique whereby two or more houses are built in a line and share one wall in common. This mode of construction underwent a formalization away from the traditional façade and into a Neoclassical mold, under the

fig. 27

22 (background screen). Traditional Scottish-Irish design house; engraving of the home of the poetess, Felicia Hemans, near St. Asaph, Wales, pre-1850.
24b (left, middle). The David Crabill House, grounds of the C. J. Brown Reservoir, built ca. 1826.
26 (left, bottom). The "Dr. Nehls" House, Rt. 41 & U.S. Rt. 42, South Charleston, Ohio, built ca. 1830.
27 (above). Buena Vista Tavern, U.S. 40 at Buena Vista Road, built ca. 1835.
28 (at left, top). J. C. Fuller House, Ohio 41 & New Carlisle-St. Paris Pike, built ca. 1846.

32 The Goodfellow House, Buena Vista Road, built ca. 1820-30.

influence of the brothers Adam, especially Robert, ca. 1775–1800.

The style was brought to America and became immensely popular with architects such as Charles Bulfinch and Asher Benjamin, who were quite influential after 1800. Benjamin and others, in many cases, produced exact duplicates of British prototypes.

Houses of this type were narrow and severe. The front door was moved to one side with two windows beside it. The doors and windows usually had flat arches with keystones, built of cut stone, which contrasted nicely with the brick walls. On the Ohio "frontier," a flat stone lintel often took the place of the arch over windows and doors. In some cases, doors had a semicircular fanlight, or panel above them, and windows often had a recessed, semicircular panel at the top *(fig. 29, at right, top)* covered with stucco. Both traits are found in the Huffman House.

Since these were originally intended to be town houses of the row type, they had party walls of masonry which was commonly carried up to the ridge of the roof, or nearly so. This supporting brickwork at each end allowed the house to have four rooms upstairs with fireplaces (two at each end), and four downstairs. Each chimney would thus have to serve for only two flues. These connected chimneys are now known as "bridged chimneys" and it was the concept of the high party wall supporting the chimneys that made the design so important, by providing extra space in the house without a complex flue system to heat it.

Once the design was firmly established in Philadelphia, Boston and elsewhere, it was but a short step to the idea of extracting a single house from a row and setting it down in the Ohio countryside. It was also quickly found that a one-story version, or a two-story with a shallow gable roof, could often get by without the bridging masonry. Thus, especially in the one-story variety, both forms of the design are found in this area.

The interiors of these homes were usually finished in the same manner as the "Virginia" type. The Ohio frontier, of course, had little use for the elaborate plaster work often found in eastern versions of these houses. However, neatly paneled doors and other well-finished woodwork were used quite commonly.

The "Pennsylvania" style, as well as the "Virginia" on occasion, was susceptible to one other variation—the "bank" form. Just as barns and houses in the Pennsylvania countryside were often built against a hillside, thereby necessitating several levels to the structure, so also were houses built in Ohio. This eliminated excavating a cellar and sometimes a spring could be incorporated into the lowest level for drinking, washing and refrigeration. This was the original multi-level house, but we graciously call it "Pennsylvania Bank style."

29 (above). Design for a town house by Asher Benjamin, in the Federal style, from his book, The American Builder's Companion, 1827.
31 (below). The Hunt Homestead, "Simon Kenton Farm," 1832; the house supposedly required 153,000 bricks, costing $6.00/ thousand, fired and laid.
32 (at left). The Goodfellow House, Buena Vista Road, south of U.S. 40, built ca. 1820–30.

31 *The Hunt Homestead, "Simon Kenton Farm," 1832*

33 *Federal style residence in New Carlisle at 106 E. Jefferson Street.*

Some of the well-known local landmarks in these styles include: the Erter Homestead, (Virginia Bank style) ca. 1829, Home Road & North Belmont Avenue (fig. 30, right); the Hunt Homestead, 1832, Rt. 68 near the Navistar Plant (fig. 31, previous page); the Goodfellow House, ca. 1820–1830, Buena Vista Road south of U.S. 40 (fig. 32, previous page); the home at 106 East Jefferson Street, New Carlisle, notable for its pure Federal style (fig. 33, at left), and last of all is the famous Daniel Hertzler House in George Rogers Clark Park, ca. 1854 (fig. 34, right, bottom). The latter features a slightly muted Late Federal façade with free-standing chimneys and Bank style ground plan.

As can be easily seen, from the above dates, both the "Virginia" and "Pennsylvania" styles of Late Federal architecture were extremely durable. They remained popular for rural dwellings up to the 1850s, although towns were experiencing changes. With the arrival of the National Road in Springfield in the 1830s, there was also the coming of many new people. Some of these were from eastern cities or urban areas and were well familiar with the newer styles of architecture. They would gently nudge Springfield into new building designs.

30 (immediately below). The Erter House, North Belmont at Home Road, probably built by Jeremiah Warder, ca. 1829.
33 (at left). Federal style residence in New Carlisle located at 106 E. Jefferson Street.
34 (at bottom). The Daniel Hertzler House, George Rogers Clark Park, built 1854–55.

30 *Erter Homestead, Home Road & North Belmont Avenue.*

34 *The Daniel Hertzler House, George Rogers Clark Park, built 1854–55.*

page 25

Greek R...

ATHENS ON...

It is ever a remarkable phenomenon the way Nature sometimes arranges a whole set of circumstances in such a favorable fashion that the germ of an idea has but to light among them and it flourishes like the most well-fertilized plant. Such is the case with what has been called the Greek Revival style of architecture.

If we except the smaller and less significant settlements of France, Spain and Holland in North America, almost all architecture employed in America from the earliest days was of English origin. In the sixteenth and seventeenth centuries, homes in the new colonies were derived from those the colonists were familiar with in the Mother Country, particularly the late Mediaeval styles of southern England ✦ *(fig. 35a, at left))*. Occasionally a variant would be found, such as the famous St. Luke's church near Smithfield, Virginia, in something of a rural, Tudor Gothic. Although in England Inigo Jones had introduced a version of the Italian Renaissance ✦ *(fig. 35b, right, top)*, and later Palladian forms would be used ✦ *(fig. 35c, right bottom)*, the colonies had neither the means nor justification for grand palaces in these styles, derived indirectly from ancient Roman forms. Still later the great period of Baroque architecture would come and go, hardly affecting England. It was unfelt by the colonies and appeared only in the distant Spanish provinces, where fantastic cathedrals would be built in this style of sensuous curving lines.

Beginning in the early eighteenth century, the colonies now had the means and population to attempt some rather pretentious buildings for public use. The Palladian form of the Renaissance style, with its characteristic arcades and central arched window, flanked by a rectangular one on either side, was still immensely popular at home and thus came to be

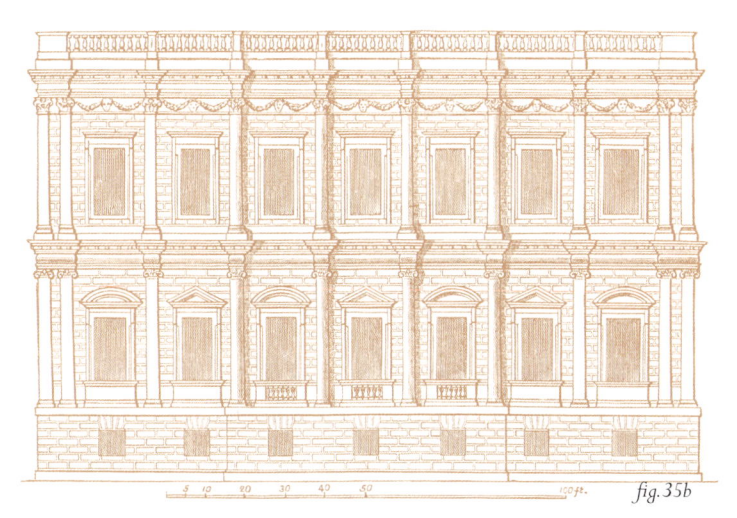

35a (at left). The Leonard House, Raynham, Massachusetts, built in 1670 on Mediaeval-Tudor lines. 35b (above). Banqueting Hall, Whitehall, London, by Inigo Jones (1573-1632). 35c (below). Library, Queen's College, Oxford University, Oxford, England, built in 1692–94 in the Palladian style.

BUCK CREEK?

chapter FOUR

36 (immediate right). Faneuil Hall, Boston; built 1742, remodeled 1805, is Palladian. Building on the left is in a much older, Mediaeval style.
39b (first inset, below). Fireplace and overmantel by Robert Adam.
38 (second inset). Birthplace of Scottish poet Robert Burns, near Ayr, Scotland. Traditional Scottish-Irish design.

adopted in the colonies with almost boring regularity (fig. 36, above). But while churches, colleges and other public buildings might be done in what was stylish architecture in England, the ordinary home was not so susceptible to change.

New Englanders had gradually modified their Mediaeval style into the "Saltbox" form (fig. 37, below) so beloved by modern real estate developers. Nevertheless, it was basically the same old house. In the middle and southern colonies the immigration of the Scottish-Irish had brought in their traditional style (fig. 38, left, below), which would remain in use well into the nineteenth century. In a few remote places it would last until the dawn of the twentieth century. Only the wealthier of planters and merchants

no place like home | athens on buck creek

could afford to build or remodel in the current Neoclassical mode, which we now call Georgian, after three of England's kings.

During the last half of the eighteenth century, there was considerable change in architecture in Great Britain. The Scottish architect Robert Adam, along with his brothers—principally James—became almost an overnight success. The exteriors of his houses were not radically different from those designed by other architects. All used the same Neoclassical approach, which meant deriving details from Roman buildings. Adam sometimes made his a bit more severe than others, sometimes a bit richer, but not totally so ❀ *(fig. 39a, right)*.

What was different was his interior treatment. Adam had studied the remains of Roman private homes at Pompeii, Herculaneum and elsewhere. It was his thesis that houses derived from Roman models should be finished on the interior like Roman private homes, not like Roman temples. He drew from the most elegant ruins then available and did not scruple to take a decorative motif and apply it to something the Romans never

37 (below and left). The Adams House, Quincy, Massachusetts, Saltbox style. 39a (above). Design for an English country villa in the Robert Adam style, much like his famous Kedleston Hall, Surrey County, England.

37 *The Adams House, Quincy, Massachusetts.*

page 29

had, such as a fireplace mantel. His great love was doing ceilings with relief work in the form of garlands, swags, rosettes etc., in plaster or stucco. Elegance, refinement and richness with restraint were all his hallmarks ✺ *(fig. 39b, previous page)*.

On the whole, the effect of Adam's work was not felt immediately in America. Notable exceptions would be George Washington's stucco ceiling at Mt. Vernon and Thomas Jefferson's unending work on Monticello. This latter probably owes more to Jefferson's own research, planning and genius than it does to Robert Adam, or anyone else.

At the conclusion of the Revolutionary War, America was ripe for rebuilding. Charles Bulfinch introduced the Adam style into Boston, and it was further popularized by Asher Benjamin. Benjamin Latrobe and other architects would utilize it in Washington, D.C., and farther south. The dominant power of the Federalist Party and its views on a strong, centralized government only served to enhance the popularity of this mode of architecture with its associations of Roman and British imperial power. But with the election of Thomas Jefferson to the presidency in 1800 was heard the first ring of the death knell of this style. Yet architectural forms do not die easily, and the further they are removed from the center of power in a country, the longer they survive. It would be well toward 1850 before the last vestiges of the Adam, or Late Federal style went to their graves in some areas.

Thomas Jefferson and his followers called themselves "Democrats." What they meant in essence was that, while they supported a central government created for the benefit of their fellow man, they also believed in the equal supremacy of state government and that elective office should not be the private domain of the wealthy or "aristocratic." Jefferson's election did not immediately affect Romanized, Neoclassical architecture; if anything, it helped it. Jefferson soon hired the brilliant Benjamin Latrobe as the architect for the Capitol. Latrobe was a dedicated classicist, but was also just as innovative as Adam. His use of tobacco leaves and ears of corn in the Capitol Building was just one strike of genius in a career of original ideas.[4]

Jefferson's party had swept the election of 1800, 1804 and every other one for many years. The appeal of the Jeffersonian philosophy is reflected in the repeat victories and hence reflects the American political mood after 1800. In an era when all scholars knew at least Latin and Greek, it was inevitable that the

---

[4]*Although Latrobe performed beautifully in Roman Neoclassical, he confessed to Jefferson that he was "a Greek at heart."*

40a *(above). The Parthenon, Athens, Greece.*
40b *(background). Greek Ionic Column.*
41b *(below). The same house design by LaFever, but in a Doric mode.*

page 31

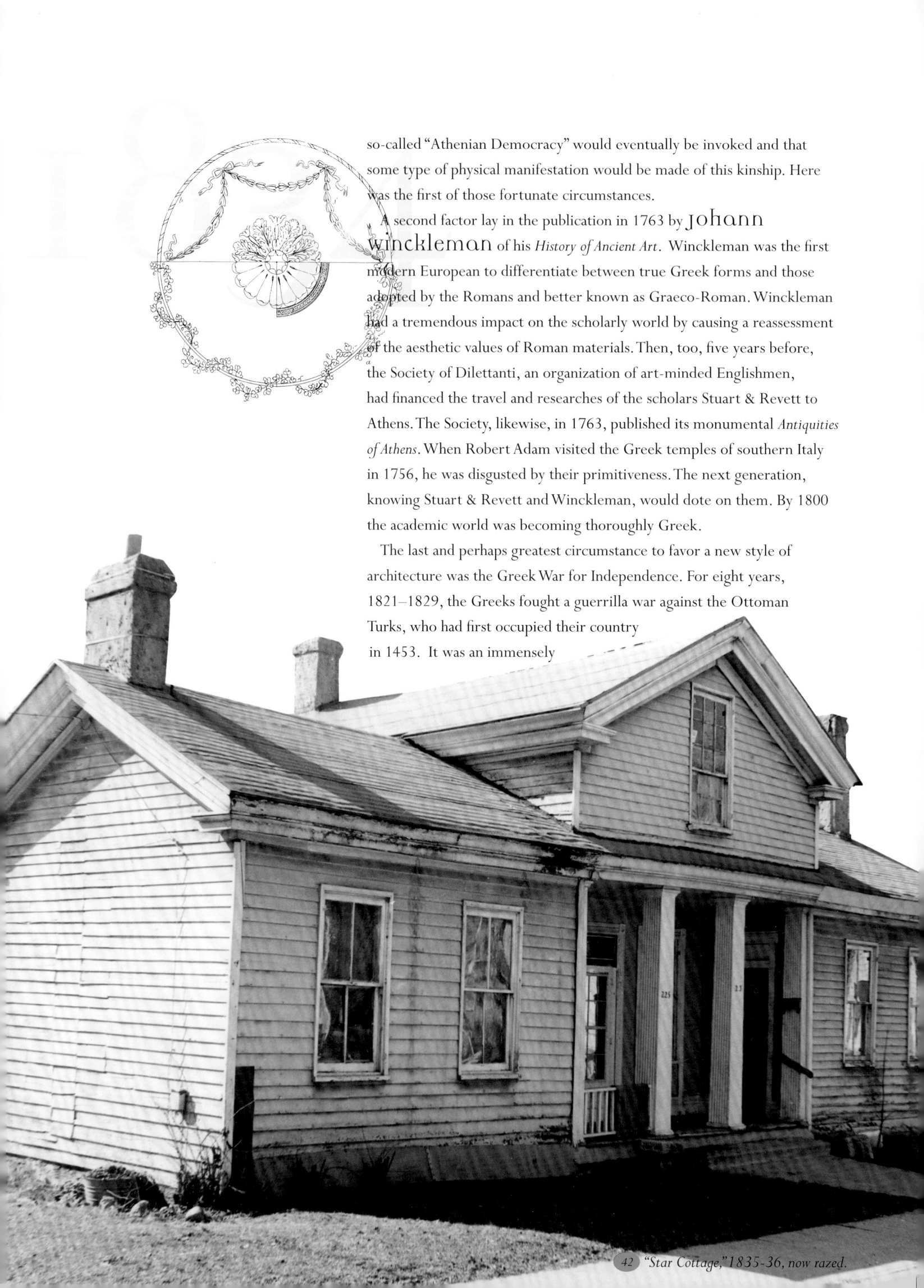

so-called "Athenian Democracy" would eventually be invoked and that some type of physical manifestation would be made of this kinship. Here was the first of those fortunate circumstances.

A second factor lay in the publication in 1763 by Johann Winckleman of his *History of Ancient Art*. Winckleman was the first modern European to differentiate between true Greek forms and those adopted by the Romans and better known as Graeco-Roman. Winckleman had a tremendous impact on the scholarly world by causing a reassessment of the aesthetic values of Roman materials. Then, too, five years before, the Society of Dilettanti, an organization of art-minded Englishmen, had financed the travel and researches of the scholars Stuart & Revett to Athens. The Society, likewise, in 1763, published its monumental *Antiquities of Athens*. When Robert Adam visited the Greek temples of southern Italy in 1756, he was disgusted by their primitiveness. The next generation, knowing Stuart & Revett and Winckleman, would dote on them. By 1800 the academic world was becoming thoroughly Greek.

The last and perhaps greatest circumstance to favor a new style of architecture was the Greek War for Independence. For eight years, 1821–1829, the Greeks fought a guerrilla war against the Ottoman Turks, who had first occupied their country in 1453. It was an immensely

42 *"Star Cottage," 1835-36, now razed.*

popular war, as wars go. The poet Lord Byron went and joined the Greeks but lost his only hope of a hero's death by succumbing to measles in an army camp in 1824. By the end of the struggle, the Greeks had won a war strikingly similar to the American War for Independence[5] and every American wanted a Greek temple for his home, office or factory. Democratic Americans had to have Democratic reminders.

Thus a number of different factors—political philosophy, kinship by precedent, art appreciation and war—combined to create an atmosphere most conducive to the development of a new architectural style: Greek Revival. There was, perhaps, one further factor, boredom. As one author has remarked, until the nineteenth century, England knew no architecture other than Roman or Gothic, alternating with each other over the centuries. It was time for a change.

One day in 1834, a 41-year-old doctor traveling by stagecoach stopped in Springfield while the horses were being changed, probably at Werden's Hotel. Having nothing else to do, he strolled down Limestone and then Spring Street to view the Indian mounds. They were situated where the railroad tracks would later cross Spring Street, before the latter was elevated.

After exhausting his interest in the mounds, he continued on, crossing Mill Run and gradually ascending the Spring Street Hill. Upon reaching the summit he was so delighted with the view and the land in general that he quickly arranged to buy a large tract, the area now bounded by Monroe, Gallagher, Selma and Spring Streets.

The doctor's name was Berkley Gillett, pronounced jill-ut, with the accent on the first syllable *(fig. 40, at right)*. He was born November 10, 1792 in either New York state, or Vermont, the fifth of ten children born to John and Rhoda Avery Gillett. The father was a farmer and Berkley had the usual Lincolnesque type of youth of hard manual labor, with but moments snatched here and there for reading and study. He was eventually able to attend the Medical University of Vermont and became a physician. In 1813 he married one Susan Crossman at Clarendon, Vermont, and then moved to North Chili, New York, to set up a practice. Dr. Gillett with his wife and four children moved to Springfield the year following his land purchase. They temporarily rented a house on Spring Street in what would later become the railroad corridor of Springfield.

We do not know what brought Dr. Gillett to Springfield, originally. Perhaps it was the ever-increasing westward migration of the 1830s. Whatever the reason, it was fortunate for Springfield. During the first year

[5] *Curiously enough, after their victory the Greeks did not reestablish a democracy, but opted for a constitutional monarchy and invited the Bavarian, Otto I, to be king.*

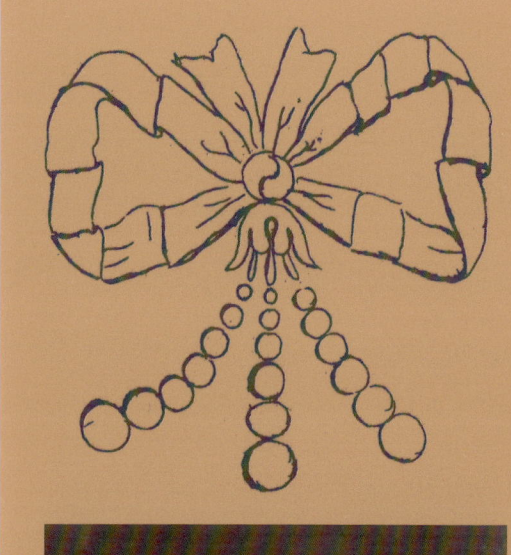

40 (above). Dr. Berkley Gillett, (1792–1855).
42 (at left). "Star Cottage," 1835–36, moved to the southwest corner of Pleasant and Vine Streets, Springfield, Ohio, now razed.

of the family's residence, while living in the rented house, the doctor was having an "artistic" cottage built on the hill in his newly acquired land. The new house was named "Star Cottage," and apparently was occupied in 1836.

Architects and builders of the Greek Revival school had three basic sources on which to draw for inspiration: the Greek temples in southern Italy, the Parthenon *(fig. 40a, page 31)* and the Erechtheum at Athens. The latter two were preferred due to their refinement. The Parthenon was done in the Doric mode, which featured a rectangular building with the entrance on either short side. The entrance consisted of a *portico* or porch with a series of columns supporting a triangular pediment. The style gave the impression of great strength and dignity.

The Erechtheum was in the more graceful and delicate Ionic style. This was characterized by taller columns than the Doric, with much carved enrichment of the column tops, or capitals, as well as the building itself *(fig. 40b, page 31)*. In smaller buildings of either style, the outside supporting columns might be eliminated and the end walls on either side of the entrance extended to act like columns, to support the pediment. These projections were called *antae*. In some cases the portico was altogether eliminated and the columns imitated by shallow projections along the front walls. These are called *pilasters*. The Erechtheum is a peculiar building because it is not only rectangular, but also has an additional porch added to one of the long sides, the famous "Porch of the Maidens." This made the building asymmetrical and has puzzled generations of scholars. Some early investigators, as well as some modern ones, consider the building as unfinished, and that it was supposed to have a corresponding porch on the other side.

This drive to find symmetry in the structure resulted in some architects designing Greek Revival houses like symmetrical Erechtheums.

This gave the impression of a building with the principal entrance on the long side, rather than on the short side, as was usual *(fig. 41a, below; 41b, page 31)*. The new cottage was built in frame, rather than stone, the traditional Greek material, and had two square columns made of boards, rather than standard round columns. The Ionic capitals of the columns were likewise replaced with simple, wooden moldings. The other wood moldings along the eaves completed the "Grecian" motif of the house. These deviations were quite the practice among American cottage builders. The practice was roundly criticized by Alexis de Tocqueville in his famous tour of America. He greatly lamented the cheap, sham wooden temples painted white which lined the Hudson River!

It is impossible to know today why Dr. Gillett chose this particular design. We may speculate, however, that Greek Revival in general was a natural choice for him, since he was from the New England area. This part of the United States, with its traditional ideas of freedom and independence had been very quick to adopt this new architectural fashion, which agreed so well with its philosophy. Dr. Gillett was doubtless prepared mentally to find this a congenial style for a new house.

"Star Cottage" stood on its hill until 1851 when the doctor decided to erect a larger house. It was moved down to the corner of Pleasant and Vine Streets *(fig. 42, previous page)*. The grand new house was enjoyed by its builder for a mere four years. Dr. Gillett died October 9, 1855, after intense suffering. The doctor's widowed second wife lived there until her death in 1872. In modern times Star Cottage was razed.

41a. Design for an Ionic Greek Revival house, by Minard LaFever, from his book, The Modern Builder's Guide, 1833.

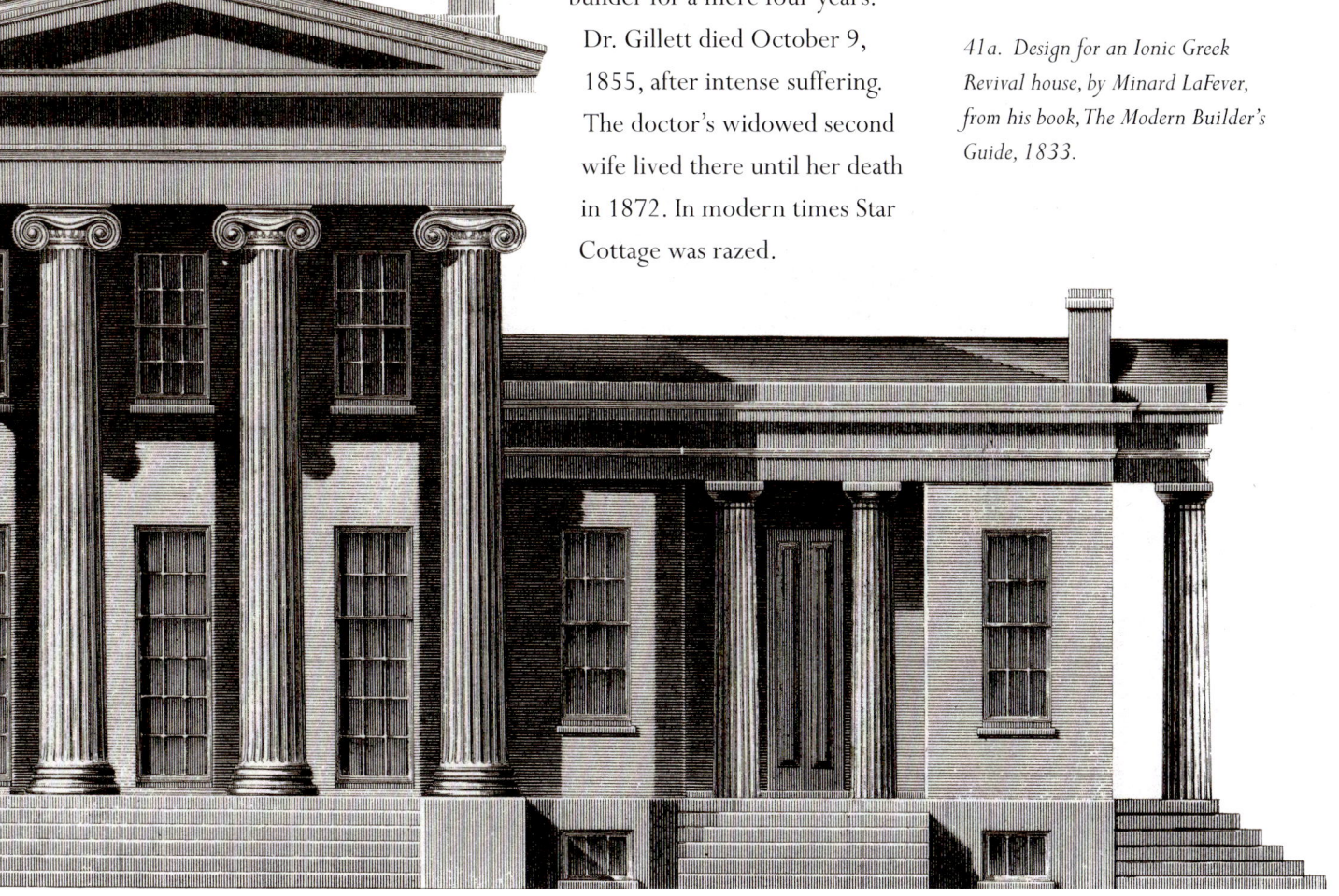

Greek

RISE AND FALL OF

Ancient Athens and Springfield, Ohio have two things in common. Each had a small, clear running stream meandering through the town. In Athens it was the Illisus Creek; in Springfield it was Mill Run Creek. In both cities the streams became polluted and eventually had to be covered over as sewers. There the similarities between the two cities end.

Although we may play the pleasant game of second-guessing Dr. Gillett's motive for building a Greek Revival cottage, it is clear that, on the whole, this architecture did not radically affect Springfield. A few more cottages and homes, such as the Weldon House *(fig. 43, next page)*, were built, or remodeled, but most Greek Revival in the area was pedestrian, at best. A wealthy Nicholas Biddle might proclaim in Philadelphia that, "The two great truths in the World are the Bible and Grecian architecture," and then add a whole Parthenon front to his home in 1836. Such was not done in Springfield, Clark County, Ohio.

Americans had basically three choices open to them when they chose to build in the Grecian style. One, they could construct or remodel a building in what is now called an "archaeologically correct" style. That is, after the architect had successfully studied the various books such as Stuart & Revett, Winckleman and particularly a volume by the British architect Nicholson, entitled simply *Architecture*, he could design a building which exhibited all of the external parts and decorations of a Parthenon or Erechtheum. Second, they could remodel only a portion of an existing structure so as to give at least something of the external appearance of a Greek building. This is what Nicholas Biddle did to his eighteenth-century farm manor. He added a front portico designed by Thomas U. Walter, later architect of the Capitol, which was a splendid copy of a Parthenon-type façade. Such remodeling varied tremendously in accuracy and detail. Much depended on whether a true architect was involved, or just a local carpenter-contractor working from a handbook. The third choice was to build in a modified design. Before proceeding further, let us pause for a moment and reflect on the essential qualities of the Greek temple form and how they suited American tastes and conditions.

fig. 46

44a (left). Ionic residence of Joseph Bowers, Ithiel Town, architect. Northampton, Massachusetts, ca. 1830. 44b (background screen). Corinthian style residence of S. Russell, Town & Davis, architects, Middletown, Connecticut, ca. 1831. 46 (above). Myers Hall, Wittenberg University; Doric portico, 1916.

A GREEK EMPIRE

chapter FIVE

The normal ancient Greek temple was an oblong or rectangular structure. It had an inner chamber, or two, which was surrounded on all sides by a series of columns. These columns supported the roof, which projected some distance beyond the walls of the inner chamber. Sometimes there were two rows of columns which made very deep side and front porches. The entrance was usually on a short side, or end. The roofs were of the gable variety, but the pitch was not nearly as steep as in buildings constructed for a northern climate where there is considerable rain and snow.

Three types of columns could be employed, depending on the design of the tops. The Doric style of column and temple produced a building that was relatively low, massive and strong. The Ionic gave a taller, loftier and more airy type of building. The exterior ornamentation of the Doric was rather restrained, but the Ionic *(fig. 44a, previous page)* reveled in rich carving.

In America, the use of one style or another quite often rested on two very different factors: geography and social structure. For northern areas where rain and snow were abundant, the Doric was commonly utilized. It produced lower ceilings and thus made buildings easier to heat.

Then too, the Doric was synonymous with the purest ideas of Periclean democracy in Athens. This was an ideal congenial to the independent nature of the northern areas of the United States.

On the other hand, the Ionic was not only associated with the beautiful Erechtheum, but with its period of construction, the last quarter of the fifth century B.C. This was an era considered not only luxurious, but even rather corrupt. In addition, the style was also associated with its true place of origin, the voluptuous Greek lands on the coast of Asia Minor. These several aspects of the Ionic style made it perfectly suitable for the southern states. The height that could be achieved by using Ionic columns neatly facilitated the high ceilings so necessary to the hot climate of the South. Its richness of decoration also suited the tastes of an area which had always been aristocratic in nature and where many plantations were small, luxurious kingdoms in their own right.

It is almost superfluous to note that the above are broad generalities and do not hold universally. Many Doric plantation houses exist in the South and many Ionic mansions in the North. Personal wealth, taste and education often circumvented all other considerations.

We have heretofore avoided the fact that there was a third style of Greek column, the Corinthian. This was of approximately the same height and proportions as the Ionic, but used a capital on the column that was even richer. It had the appearance of a basket with numerous leaves sprouting from and around it. The Corinthian, however, had just begun to develop in Greece's classical period. It was thus generally avoided for Greek Revival houses, except for a wealthy plantation mansion here and

fig. 43

43 (top). *The Weldon House, Rice St., Springfield, Ohio, ca. 1830–35, now razed.* 45 (bottom). *The Evans House, South Charleston, Ohio, later Greek Revival with recessed side entrance porch, ca. 1851.* 47 (at left). *Newspaper reprint of an old photograph of the original King Building, southeast corner of Main and Limestone Sts., Springfield, Ohio, constructed ca. 1850.*

fig. 45

47 *The original King Building, ca. 1850.*

page 39

there in the South. It was the Romans who truly perfected the style and thus it was used chiefly in banks and government buildings. Perhaps the most famous American home of the early nineteenth century that made use of the style was the residence of S. Russell at Middletown, Connecticut, built in 1831. Although constructed in the Greek Revival era, it had much Roman influence, especially in its high foundation, or *podium* ✺ *(fig. 44b, page 37).*

Ohio, of course, was almost a "border state." It was settled by immigrants from the North and South, as well as the Middle Atlantic States. As such, there was every degree of opinion on every subject. Then, too, the climate was not so severe as to preclude one style of architecture in favor of another. Finally, there was every degree of wealth. The result is that one can find every form of Greek Revival architecture somewhere in the state. Clark County, Springfield its seat, and its villages all show, however, a feeling strictly for the Doric, to judge from what remains. While this could be attributed by political scientists to a strong passion for democracy by the yeoman and middle class of a newly settled area, there is perhaps a much simpler explanation.

The Clark County area, like most in the United States before the Civil War, did not have native, professionally trained architects. The first American professional would be H. H. Richardson, when he returned from France in 1868. In semirural and rural districts, construction was in the hands of carpenter-contractors, who worked either from tradition or handbooks printed in eastern cities. For them, the easiest type of house to construct was the traditional, gable type. Yet a gable house could be made into a Greek Revival by simply moving the entrance from the long to the short side and the chimneys vice versa. Then, all that was necessary were wooden moldings to mark off the triangular gable end as the *pediment* of the Grecian house. The effect was completed by adding a brick or wooden pilaster at each corner of the façade. Fashion was satisfied!

While it is true that Dr. Gillett's cottage approximated in miniature some of the Ionic style mansions prescribed in architecture books, a close examination shows that it was constructed in the Doric Vernacular mode. In essence, it was nothing but one of these modified gable houses inserted crossways into a long, one-story cottage. The columns in its porch did not even carry a true pediment. They were purely decorative and served merely to fill in an area where the wall of the one-story part was cut away to allow for an entrance to the two-story part. While it was quaint and

Figure 48 (background screen, above). Model design for a Greek Revival residence, from Catherine Beecher's Treatise on Domestic Economy, edition of 1846.

49 *Greek Revival cottage, 327 S. Center Street, Springfield, Ohio, apparently built by O. S. Kelly when still a carpenter, ca. 1849–52. Note slender pilasters at corners.*

charming, Dr. Gillett's cottage was also a sham. In time such deception was abandoned and a true house form developed. The columns and the second-story quasi-pediment were eliminated, leaving a simple cottage with a recessed entry on one side, such as the former Evans House in South Charleston, built in 1851 ✶ *(fig. 45, page 39)*.

In short, then, the available relics of the Greek Revival period in Clark County show that the "archaeologically correct" mode of building was rarely, if ever, tried here. Only three public buildings were ever considered for the idea: a proposed portico for Myers Hall at Wittenberg University, which was not built until 1916 ✶ *(fig. 46, page 37)*; a second courthouse proposed for High Street, which was never built, and was more Roman than Greek; and Linden Hall Academy at New Carlisle, which was not pure Grecian. However, one commercial structure, the "Old King Building," constructed about 1850 at Main and Limestone Streets, was truly remarkable in that it employed the Greek "triglyph and metope" with *mutules* decoration under the pediment ✶ *(fig. 47, page 38)*. It was demolished in 1890 in favor of the newer Gotwald Building, which, in turn, was razed in modern times.

As to the idea of remodeling all or part of an earlier structure into Greek Revival, there are a few examples in the area. The most famous is the Myers Hall portico mentioned above. Soon after the college was opened, engravings showed the building with an Ionic portico of six columns and a flat-roofed pediment. Later this was changed in the pictures to four columns and a gabled roof. When finally built in 1916, the Ionic columns were changed to Doric positioned on Ionic bases, with a pedimented roof. The result, however, was just the same: a Late Federal Vernacular style building with a Greek Revival porch.

50 (top, right). Commercial Building, Main and Spring Streets, ca. 1850.
51 (below). Commercial Building, built by S. G. Moler, East Main Street, Springfield, Ohio, ca. 1852, now razed.
52 (third from top, right). Greek Revival Farmhouse, 2955 Mumper Rd., Harmony Township, Clark County, Ohio.
53 (second from top, right). Oliver Clark House, between Wittenberg & Lowry Streets, south of the Little Miami Railroad, ca. 1858, now razed.
55 (bottom, right). Greek Revival residence, Church and Jefferson Streets, New Carlisle, Ohio, ca. 1850.

fig. 51

The old Reid farm on South Bird Road is another example. About 1846 James Reid added an entire new front wing in vernacular Greek Revival to the old "Virginia"-style homestead. The new section is now obscured by an even more modern two-story portico.

Generally speaking, it was reserved for the twentieth century to remodel earlier homes into the Grecian style. This was usually accomplished by adding a two-story portico along one side of the house. Unfortunately the columns employed are commonly much too attenuated for their height and the porches are much too shallow to provide any great amount of shade. Shade, by the way, and shelter from rain, was the principal reason that impelled the ancient Greeks to devise and perfect the temple porch, or portico. When these two qualities are missing, so also is 50 percent of any reason for the existence of the porch.

On the whole, then, most Clark Countians chose to build, when they attempted Greek Revival, in a modified design, or "vernacular" mode. The only major question that faced such a prospective builder was just how far he would go in attempting to achieve the "Grecian mode." An extremely popular book at the time, Catherine E. Beecher's *Treatise on Domestic Economy*, (1842 and thereafter) illustrated what she considered a practical and utilitarian form of such a house ✻ *(fig. 48, background screen, page 40)*. It is, in fact, almost elaborate by this area's standards.

Although Miss Beecher places only pilasters on the front of her design, instead of true columns, local builders appear to have quickly abandoned even that concession in favor of a simpler façade with, at most, a pilaster at each corner ✻ *(fig. 49, pages 40–41)*. Even this minor concession to ornamentation was soon dropped in favor of a stark façade with two windows and a door on the first floor, three on the second ✻ *(fig's. 50, 52, & 53, at right; 51, at left, bottom)*.

It soon became apparent, however, that if the center columns or pilasters were eliminated, then the horizontal base line of the pediment appeared out of place and even seemed to sag. Thus another cut was made and the pediment line extended in only a short way from the eaves—only enough to cover the corner pilaster. Then, in quick succession, the corner pilaster was viewed as superfluous, since it no longer truly seemed to support anything. The pilaster was therefore removed, leaving only the short segment of the cornice as a decorative element ✻ *(fig's. 54, next page, & 55, at right)*. That architectural fragment has nowadays lost all connection with Greek Revival architecture and is usually just called an "eaves return."

By the above outlined series of steps, the Greek Revival style of architecture was reduced to a mere shadow of itself and the

fig. 50

fig. 53

fig. 52

fig. 55

no place like home | rise and fall of a greek empire

vernacularizing process completed. The result was a whole generation of nondescript houses whose only claim to validity was a floor plan and an exterior coat of white paint. By the end of the period, the lure of the traditional homestead had overcome many, and the newly built houses of ca. 1845–1850 often reverted to a steeper, pitched roof, entrance on the long side and only the partial pediment on the short sides.

In ancient times, both the western, as well as the eastern or Greek portion of the Roman Empire, gave way at last to invasions by peoples we call Goths. By 1850, although Greek Revival was still being built in Clark County, a new Gothic invasion was imminent: Gothic Revival architecture.

54 *The so-called "Dr. Riley House," Spring Street and Selma Road, Springfield, Ohio, ca. 1850.*

GETTING TO

On the fifth of March in 1751, Frederick Louis, Prince of Wales and heir to the throne of Great Britain, was supervising the planting of a tree at Kew Gardens. Although it was raining and nasty out-of-doors, the stubborn streak in Frederick's Hanoverian ancestry kept him at the site until the job was done. He quickly came down with pleurisy and shortly thereafter he died.

A *post mortem* on Prince Frederick indicated that the pleurisy had not been the direct cause of death; rather, it had aggravated a longstanding condition that resulted in a sudden and massive pulmonary hemorrhage. Frederick's death not only affected subsequent British and American politics, but may have affected architecture as well.

At the time of his illness, Frederick was involved in supervising the transplanting of a tree in what could be called a "naturalistic" or "picturesque" landscape ✻ *(fig. 56a, background screen)*. After centuries of domination by foreign styles of gardening, English horticulture had begun to break away from the formal gardens that had been the rule since the Middle Ages. The earliest of these had been the small gardens enclosed in monastic cloisters. Later had come the various modes popularized in Renaissance Italy, then Holland and finally the fantasies of Versailles ✻ *(fig. 56b, at right)*. But exotic, imported plants and gardening styles, brought from the New World and Asia in the seventeenth century, began to change things.

By the early 1700s, advanced English thinkers had accepted the thesis that Nature should not be constrained within a particular pattern. Rather, the gardener should aim to assist, or "enhance" Nature by the most careful clearing and planting of sites. Woods should have proper paths and open here and there to give certain views, or "vistas." Flowers and special trees should also be planted to highlight a particular view, or stand out as interesting specimens. Prince Frederick was an aesthete who could appreciate this thinking, unlike his father (King George II) and his son (who would be King George III) who were extremely conventional, if not plodding.

fig. 56b

56a (background screen). A "picturesque" landscape of the 1840s, with Gothic Revival cottage, from Downing's Architecture.
56b (above). A formal garden in the "Geometric style" of the Elizabethan period, from Downing's Landscape Gardening.
72 (at left). A Gothic cottage, originally located at South Fountain Avenue and Pleasant Streets, later moved to Route 68 north of Yellow Springs, Ohio.

THE POINT

chapter SIX

Along with this theory of appreciating an enhanced Nature came an interest in the Gothic ruins that dotted the British countryside. They, if nothing else, certainly highlighted the landscape. Soon ruined abbeys, monasteries and castles came to be viewed as extremely valuable horticultural adjuncts to any estate ✺ *(fig. 57, below)*. Shrouded in vegetation, and mystery, these venerable piles of stone became the inspiration for innumerable literary works, as well as sources for decorative, architectural motifs. Had Prince Frederick lived and become King, royal interest might have greatly facilitated a Gothic Revival much earlier. As it was, the Gothic Revival, in its early stages, had to smolder beneath the surface of eighteenth-century Neoclassicism. Only now and then did it burst forth in a spectacular tongue of flame.

Perhaps the earliest of these Gothic eruptions was in the person of Horace Walpole, son of Prime Minister Sir Robert Walpole. Horace was a dilettante in everything and much addicted to trivia. He refused to be serious about anything. In 1749 he began to remodel an old coachman's house into his conception of a

Gothic mansion. The house, which he called "Strawberry Hill" ✺ *(fig. 58, at right)*, was like him—rather frivolous. Yet it remains the first such attempt in England and became, perhaps inadvertently, the only serious thing in his life. He worked on the mansion for the next 43 years, ever building and remodeling. His contemporary, the great furniture designer and builder Thomas Chippendale, published his *The Gentleman and Cabinet-maker's Director* in 1754. In this landmark work, many pieces of furniture reflected not only the popular Rococo style, but also the Chinese and Gothic. Chippendale's Gothic ✺ *(fig. 59. right, below)*, however, was like Walpole's: a trifle fanciful.

The greatest of the eighteenth-century Gothic flashes was WILLIAM BECKFORD. Born in 1760, the son of a Lord Mayor of London, he was an erratic genius from childhood, stimulated by the greatest fortune in England. His youth, replete with sexual scandals and gossip, forced him into an early marriage, but his wife died only three years later. He traveled extensively to escape persecution, but was never acceptable to Society.

In 1799 he began to construct on the site of his family's old country house, "Fonthill." This new mansion would outdo anything in England, especially Walpole's "Strawberry Hill." The new house, called "Fonthill Abbey," was not finished until 1807. It had eighteen bedrooms, a seventy-two-foot gallery and a dominating tower, one hundred forty-five feet in height! In 1813 Beckford lost interest in the house, which he sold in 1822, and his magnificent tower collapsed in ruins on December 21, 1825. So much for preliminaries!

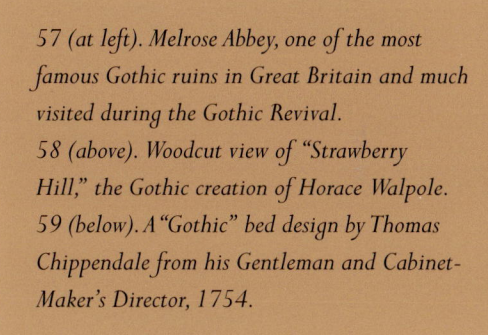

57 (at left). Melrose Abbey, one of the most famous Gothic ruins in Great Britain and much visited during the Gothic Revival.
58 (above). Woodcut view of "Strawberry Hill," the Gothic creation of Horace Walpole.
59 (below). A "Gothic" bed design by Thomas Chippendale from his Gentleman and Cabinet-Maker's Director, 1754.

57 Melrose Abbey, Great Britain.

61 *Porter's Cottage, Fairmount Park, Philadelphia, ca. 1799.*

Although a few English gentlemen of wealth could and would remodel or build a house like Walpole or Beckford, the majority declined. Many would call in a landscape designer and redo their gardens/parks *(fig. 60, background screen, below)*. Some would even go so far as to build a pseudo "Gothic Temple" on their estates. Only a few would radically alter their ancestral Tudor or Palladian country houses. It was left largely to Americans, who had no ancestry or history, to drop backwards in time and pick up the Gothic thread afresh.

Eighteenth-century Americans were, to judge from architectural remains, almost completely uninterested in Gothic design. They were quite satisfied with their formal gardens and Neoclassical houses. Only rarely does an off-pitch note sound; as usual, it was Thomas Jefferson. In 1771, during the early days of building Monticello, he planned a battlemented tower near his mansion and also a small "Gothic Temple of antique appearance." Jefferson was an ardent bibliophile and the most current English works on gardening were to be found in his library. Therefore, his unexecuted designs are quite predictable.

Other than Jefferson's scheme, virtually nothing Gothic was built in America until 1799. That year the architect Benjamin Henry Latrobe arrived in America and soon had a commission for a Gothic house from William Hammond of Philadelphia, where by 1800 there was a Gothic porter's lodge at Fairmount Park *(fig. 61, at left)*. It was not until after 1820, however, that Gothic structures began to be built with any frequency. This was largely due to the increasing popularity of the mediaeval novels of Sir Walter Scott and the romantic productions of the Hudson River School of Romantic painting. Before 1820, perhaps not more than half-a-dozen houses were constructed in America with Gothic detailing or design.

After 1820, the Gothic Revival received a devastating blow from the skyrocketing popularity of Greek Revival, yet a small number of hardy souls continued to be won over to the cause. Not the least, and perhaps the most ardent of these, was Andrew Jackson Downing.

A. J. Downing *(fig. 62, top, right)* was born in 1815 at Newburgh, New York, where he and his brother Charles eventually inherited a nursery business. Downing's youthful studies in landscape design exposed him to the popular "Picturesque" school of English gardening. Through this medium he became acquainted with Gothic Revival architecture, to which he became an immediate convert.

Downing married in 1839, taking his bride to a newly built Tudor style house *(fig. 63, right, below)* at Newburgh, one of a number of such houses that had begun to spring up in the Hudson River Valley, after 1832. Then in 1841 he published his first book, *A Treatise on the Theory and Practice of Landscape Gardening*, which was an immediate success and contained much information on Gothic and Tudor Revival architecture.

The next eleven years of his life were filled with three more

60 (screen at lower left). View at "Wellesley" estate near Boston. A formal French garden is in foreground, beyond is an English garden, from a posthumous edition of Downing's Gardening, ca. 1865. 61 (at left). Porter's Cottage, Fairmount Park, Philadelphia, ca. 1799. 62 (above). Portrait of A. J. Downing, from 1865 edition of his Landscape Gardening. 63 (below). View of "Highland Garden," the home Downing built at Newburgh, New York, in 1839, from Landscape Gardening, 1865.

65a (at top). Woodcut of a small frame cottage ornée, Downing.
65b (middle). Example of Gothic cottage praised by Downing, White Plains, New York.
65c (bottom). Downing design for country villa.

books, *Cottage Residences*, *Rural Essays*, and *The Architecture of Country Houses*. He also edited several books on horticulture, published the definitive *Fruits and Fruit Trees of America*, and also published a monthly magazine, *The Horticulturist*, from 1846–1852.

In nearly every one of his writings, Downing preached the sublime and uplifting virtues of the Gothic/Tudor Revival, as opposed to the incongruity and (like de Tocqueville) sham qualities of Grecian houses. Downing himself was scarcely an architect, but had phenomenal luck in associating with A. J. Davis, perhaps America's most talented architect of the period. Davis was completely versatile and could design in almost any mode. Among other commissions, he was one of the architects of the Ohio capitol at Columbus, in Greek Revival style. His adaptability may be due to his declaring early in life, like Horace Walpole, that he refused to take anything seriously.

Downing thus did the preaching and publishing while having Davis do the actual designs, in addition to his own professional career. Downing later took in as protégé a young, immigrant English architect, Calvert Vaux, who would eventually become one of America's leading designers.

Downing was handsome, brilliant, dynamic and, to use a modern cliché, charismatic. There was no one he could not convince and, by 1846, he could say, "The Greek Temple disease has passed its crisis…the people have survived it."

The people had had a good physician in A. J. Downing, for it was he, more than anyone else, who had breathed life back into the Gothic Revival in America.

On Wednesday afternoon, July 28, 1852, Downing and his wife were taking a pleasure cruise on a Hudson River steamboat, the *Henry Clay*. The

65a (at left, from top). Woodcut of a small frame cottage ornée, Downing, Architecture. 65b (middle). Example of the type of Gothic cottage praised by Downing. Residence of S. E. Lyon, White Plains, New York, Architecture. 65c (bottom). Design for a country villa, from Downing. 67c (immediate left). Cottage, 401 S. Yellow Springs St. Originally a Greek Revival design, it was remodeled into Gothic by the addition of "gingerbread" to the eaves of the roof and porch. Compare to figure 67a (below). Another design for vergeboards which was later much simplified into a simple swirling scroll. It could be cut on a jigsaw and was used in a variety of applications, especially on the eaves of porches, Downing. 67b (at top). Design for a gable with Gothic vergeboards, Downing.

captain decided to engage in a race with another boat, the *Armenia*. During the contest, an overheated boiler on the *Henry Clay* ignited the wooden superstructure. The craft hove into the shore ✸ *(fig. 64, right)*, but the water was very deep with no beach and many were drowning while trying to reach dry land. Downing was last seen throwing objects from the burning ship to those in the water, for them to cling to and paddle ashore. His body was washed up the following morning.

Downing and his disciples had been absorbed in propagandizing two forms of architecture: the *cottage ornée* (decorated cottage), and the Tudor Gothic Villa ✸ *(fig's. 65a, b & c, page 52)*. The former of these was intended to be of a size suitable for a single family, with perhaps one or two servants. The villa was large enough to require, in some cases, a whole corps of domestics. The floor plan of the cottage was an asymmetrical or informal grouping of rooms, as opposed to the strict symmetry of Neoclassical styles.

The fabric of the building ideally was to be dressed stone. Yet, given the difficulties of working in this medium, Downing felt that brick, coated with stucco to imitate stone, was quite acceptable. If one could not afford stone or coated brick, then frame construction was permissible, but in a particular way. Downing and Vaux both popularized vertical siding with *battens*, or wooden strips covering the joints between boards, instead of the standard, horizontal weatherboarding ✸ *(fig. 66, above, left)*. The idea, of course, was to give the house an upward thrust, visually.

The two most prominent external characteristics of the cottage ornée were the gables and the windows. The roofs of these houses were to be rather steeply pitched, with several gables to give a variety of "elevations." Furthermore, the eaves of the gables were to be fitted with boards having trefoil or quatrefoil cutouts, or Gothic tracery. Unfortunately some carpenters built structures with so many gables and "gingerbread," a corruption of the word *vergeboard*, that they were said to resemble laced, cocked hats. Extremely simple, wooden eaves brackets were also recommended. With the popularization of curving lines in the Rococo styles of the 1850s and 1860s, the vergeboards became scroll or vine-like

64 (inset, top). Woodcut illustration of the "Henry Clay" disaster, July 28, 1852, from Gleason's Pictorial Drawing Room Companion. 66 (above). Design for a Gothic cottage-villa using vertical siding and battens. Downing, Architecture. 69a (at right, bottom). House on North Plum Street with pseudo-Gothic gable, razed in the spring of 1977. 69b (at right, top). Residence, North Chillicothe Street, South Charleston, with Carpenter style gable and lancet window. 70 (background screen). View of William Paulding's house, "Lyndhurst," before being enlarged by Jay Gould. The house was built in 1838 from A. J. Davis' designs. Downing, Architecture.

69b) *Residence, North Chillicothe Street, South Charleston.*

69a) *House on North Plum Street with pseudo-Gothic gable.*

page 55

cutouts, done with jigsaws ✶ *(fig's. 67a & b, page 53)*.

The windows of these cottages were to be of either of two forms. They could be tall and pointed—*lancet* windows—or rectangular with a framework across the top and down about one-third of the sides. This frame was known as a Tudor *label* ✶ *(fig. 68, inset, below, left)*. The lancet form often underwent considerable modification at the hands of unsophisticated carpenters. Where shops that could properly fabricate the point on the window frame were lacking, carpenters commonly substituted a simple, triangular top, rather than the gentle curve. In a few cases a *label* was attempted, although it should have been reserved for the rectangular Tudor style. The triangular top was particularly popular in rural areas, where older houses were commonly remodeled by simply adding a dormer to the long side of the roof and therein adding the modified window ✶ *(fig's. 69a & b, previous page)*.

The Gothic Villa, or country house, could take two forms. It could be but an enlarged and slightly more formal cottage design, or it might incorporate details of Elizabethan period mansions. In the latter case, although the decorative motifs gave the usual upward thrust, there was also a striving for horizontality. The horizontal effect also made the house seem more a part of the natural landscape (Frank Lloyd Wright would strive for the same thing much later), but also gave the feeling of an old house to which additions had been made over the centuries. The most famous of these villas in America was designed by Davis in 1838 for

71 (below). Vignette of "Oakfield," Dr. John Ludlow's residence on East High Street beyond the city limits. Taken from the 1852 (aerial drawing) View of Springfield.
73 (above). Gothic Revival cottage, 321 South Yellow Springs Street.
74 (at far right). Gothic Revival cottage, 325 South Yellow Springs Street, with an Italianate porch.
68 (inset, above). Gothic window design from Downing, combining pointed, lancet window insert within a Tudor framework and label.

74 *Gothic Revival cottage, 325 South Yellow Springs Street.*

William Paulding at Tarrytown, New York ✦ *(fig. 70, screen on page 54)*. It was later acquired by the "robber baron" financier, Jay Gould, and enlarged. This remodeling was fortunately done with extremely good taste in a style that perfectly harmonized with Davis' original design. The property now belongs to The National Trust and is known as "Lyndhurst."

To judge from available remains, the Gothic Revival enjoyed moderate popularity in Springfield and Clark County. The truest, most Downingesque house was the then rural home of John Ludlow, "Oakfield," ✦ *(fig. 71, page 56)* located on East High Street at the present Ludlow Avenue, now the site of a church. Another fine example is the frame cottage once located at South Fountain Avenue and Pleasant Street and moved to the Yellow Springs area some years ago ✦ *(fig. 72, page 46)*.

Perhaps the two houses that are still standing and show the greatest amount of Gothic Revival detail are the homes at 321 and 325 South Yellow Springs Street ✦ *(fig's. 73 & 74, previous page)*. Both of these are rather late for the style, having been built ca. 1867–1868. The one at 325 has the better windows of the two, although the other, while employing the triangular top, does utilize an almost Tudor label. The floor plans of both, however, are quite typical of the late 1860s and early 1870s vernacular houses. In addition, their roofs are not nearly as steeply pitched as they should be for Gothic Revival.

Here and there throughout the older sections of Springfield are scattered houses with a touch of the style, principally confined to a second floor window ✦ *(fig. 75, below)*. Many, doubtless, had more detailing at one time, but decay and remodeling have taken their toll. One of the most delightful was the Thomas House at the corner of East High and York Streets. Stripped of its woodwork and with a modern addition, it now conveys hardly any Gothic image at all ✦ *(see figures 76a & b, at right)*.

75 *House on West Columbia Street with Gothic gables and lancet window in attic, now razed.*

76a (above). John H. Thomas House, 709 East High Street, built 1853, from Springfield Illustrated, 1889.

76b (below). A contemporary photograph of the John H. Thomas House.

page 59

77 *The O. S. Kelly House, ca. 1868, 403 South Fountain Avenue, contemporary photograph.*

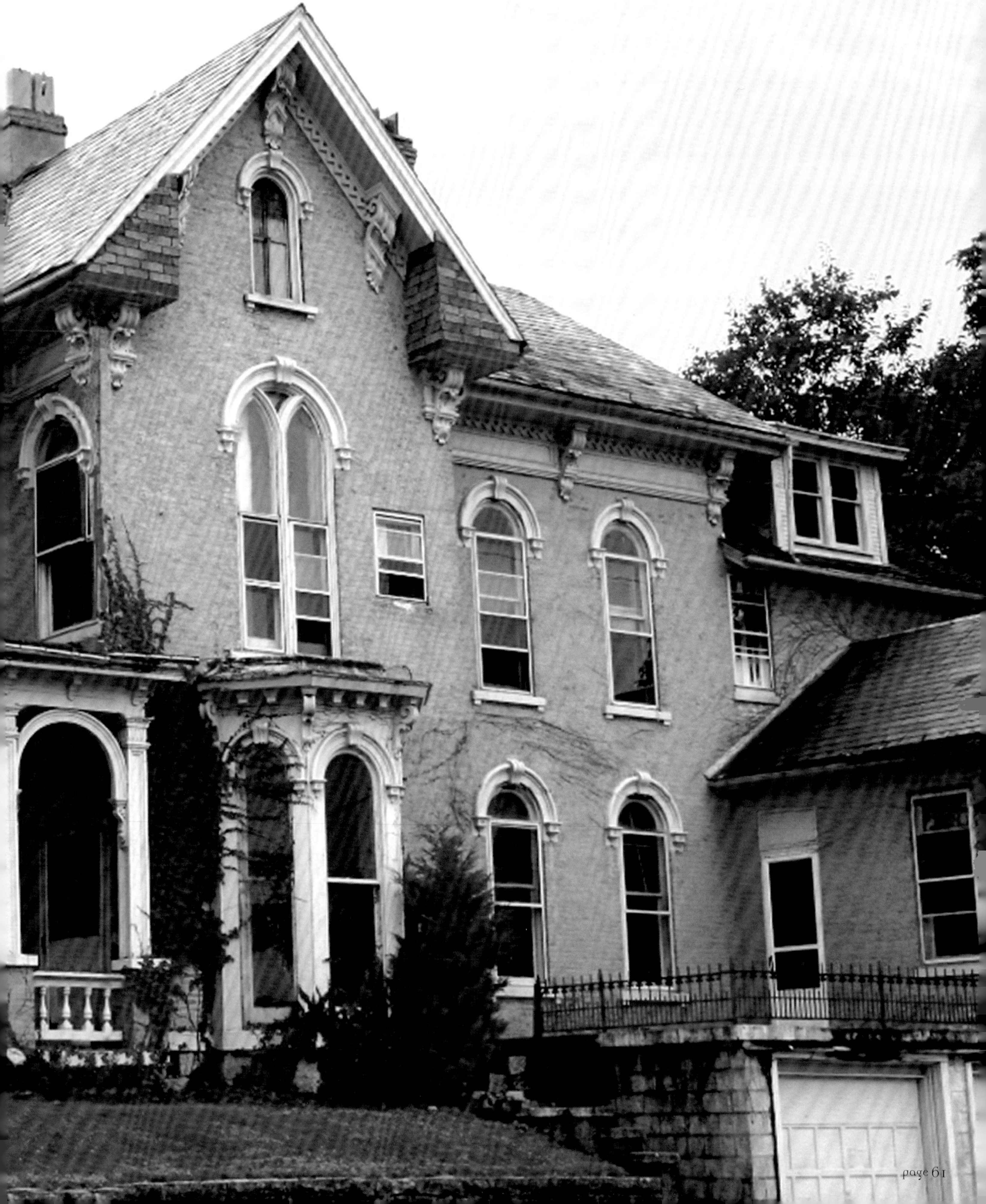

An interesting variant on the style is the house in which O. S. Kelly finally settled (fig. 77, previous page) in 1868. Although it is an eclectic, asymmetrical vernacular house, it does have some excellent Gothic Revival about it. So also a house at Wittenberg and Jefferson Streets, which had the unusual feature of a lancet window with tracery crossed with a rounded Italianate to produce a handsome hybrid (fig. 78, below).

The Tudor/Gothic Revival Villa seems to have been completely ignored by local builders, or there was simply no demand at the time. When the demand did finally arise, the style was available and began to be utilized. This, however, did not occur until the 1890s when a rash of revivals began to occur. Thus, for Springfield they tend to be a revival of a revival. One of the most outstanding is the Kissell House on North Fountain Boulevard (see figure 224, page 180), which will be discussed later.

By the time of his death in 1852, Downing's *The Architecture of Country Houses* was already carrying several styles of architectural designs (fig. 79, screen, below) other than Gothic Revival, which was beginning to fade in popularity. It would, however, continue to be used on a limited basis until the 1870s (fig. 80, at right).

One thing that is always associated with the Revival is *gloom*. Even some contemporaries of Downing spoke lovingly about the gloom that could be produced by the style. These somewhat morbid characters did not represent Downing's own view. He and other true lovers of the Gothic were interested in the varying effects of light and shadow that could be produced by the deep eaves, varying elevations and proper landscaping. These effects were supposed to be used to induce a variety of emotions and sentiments, which was in accord with the period's emphasis on romanticism. Whether light and shadow, or pure gloom, all was soon to be dispelled by the brilliant sunshine of an Italian *intermezzo* in American architecture.

78 (above). House at Wittenberg Avenue and Jefferson Street, built late 1860s. The house was basically Italianate, but notice the Gothic window with trefoil top and cap.
79 (screen, right, below). Design for a cubic Italianate house, Downing, Architecture.
80 (at right). An 1870s Italianate house with gothic shaped gable and lancet window, 518 West High Street.

80 *An 1870s Italianate house, 518 West High Street.*

ITALIAN INTER

From the time of the Middle Ages onward, Italy and its cities, especially Rome, had been the goal of travelers from all over Europe. Until the era of the Reformation, the majority of these travelers had been religious pilgrims seeking out the famous churches, shrines and cathedrals. During and after the Reformation and its attendant wars and disturbances, the number of pilgrims declined. Yet, this void was filled with a new type of pilgrim, the architecture student. As early as 1512, Italian immigrant craftsmen settled in England, bringing with them the details of the Neoclassical form of Italian Renaissance architecture. Englishmen, like other Europeans, then began to flock to Italy, there to study the newly rediscovered glories of ancient Roman civilization.

By the middle of the eighteenth century, the wealthier English and some Americans had come to realize that there was a great deal of culture to be gained outside their rather parochial worlds. The result was the sending of sons, once they reached eighteen or thereabouts, on an extensive tour of Europe. This came to be known as the "Grand Tour." It might be prolonged for up to two years and involved lengthy stays in various cities where the young man was supposed to pursue the study of local culture. In many cases, all the young man pursued was the opposite sex and luxurious living; yet the habit became entrenched and lasted until the beginning of the twentieth century.

Although the young heirs to great fortunes visited a number of places in France and the Lowlands, their ultimate goal was a group of small kingdoms which, together with the Papal States, comprised modern day Italy. In addition to wealthy tourists, almost any sick person, whose disease was obscure and difficult to treat, was advised to take up residence in the warm, sunny climate of Italy. By 1800, even young ladies were traveling in the country, with a chaperon, of course, pursuing culture, health or possibly a wealthy husband.

82 (small background screen). Woodcut view of Florence.
83 (at left). Richard Upjohn's design for an Italian villa, built in 1845 for Edward King, of Newport, R.I.; from Downing's Architecture.
94 (below). House with rounded, Italianate windows, 417 Center St., Springfield, Ohio.

MEZZO

chapter SEVEN

With the coming of the nineteenth century and the revival of Romanticism, it was inevitable that these tourists—wealthy, well educated and influential—would sooner or later exert some influence on the designs of their future homes. The Greek Revival was the first outburst of the Romantic spirit that now rebelled against the formalism and logic of the Neoclassical. The Gothic Revival finally broke the back of the Neoclassical in killing off the Greek Revival. This, in turn, left the door open for a second school of Romantic architecture, the Italianate *(fig. 81, below)*.

The tourists who visited Italy in the eighteenth and early nineteenth centuries largely confined themselves to the upper half of the country. The farther south they went, the poorer and unhealthier they found the climate and lifestyle. Southern Italian *banditti* were notorious and only the hardiest authors, artists and architects visited the Greek ruins in the South and in Sicily. What the tourists saw mainly were Roman ruins, Romanesque and Renaissance palaces and churches, as well as country houses and Palladian villas. The principal cities visited were Rome (naturally!!), Florence, Venice, Turin, Genoa and Milan. Of these, romantic Venice and picturesque Florence *(fig. 82, screen, previous page)* seem to have exerted the greatest influence of all.

Florence in particular was well suited to the spirit of the times. Located in a beautiful valley amidst the hill country to the north of Rome, it abounded in elegant specimens of palaces and churches, as well as quaint country houses and villas. It was Florence that had particularly fine specimens of transitional Romanesque-Renaissance palaces, while Venice had outstanding high Renaissance types.

But it was the rural, middle-class type of houses that particularly caught the tourist's eye. Most of these homes had stood for several centuries already, gradually receiving numerous additions. The result was an irregular or asymmetrical mass of attached blocks and cubes, often with a lookout tower, but nothing of the formal about it.

The wide, low, hipped roofs were supported on brackets and cast shadows, giving a variety of appearances during the different hours of the day. The irregularity also provided for a number of different "elevations" to the structure. Such homes were in a completely different mode from the Gothic Revival, yet they had all the same aesthetic qualities and thus fit perfectly into the prevailing taste for an artistic house style.

fig. 86

81(below). Nineteenth-century woodcut, depicting a highly romanticized view of Italy. 84 (screen, at top). Downing's 1842 Italianate villa design. 85 (at right). Greenway Academy, as it appeared in 1852. 86 (above). The Downey House, 736 East High Street, Springfield, Ohio.

no place like home | italian intermezzo

By the mid 1840s, the irregular Italianate house had become naturalized in America and was giving the Gothic Revival heavy competition.[6] Downing, of course, did not dislike the style; he merely felt more could be accomplished architecturally, artistically and spiritually through the Gothic. And so, even Downing turned his hand at Italianates. In 1842 he produced a design for a bracketed Italianate house which became standard in his works and widely copied by others *(fig. 84, screen at top, far left)*. This design does have a particular advantage over Upjohn's. Except for the arched opening in the tower and attic, all of the windows are square or rectangular. This was, archaeologically, the correct form for a rural Italianate. What Upjohn had done was to employ eclecticism, or the borrowing of motifs from several different sources for use in one final product.

The influence of Downing's standard design was felt all across the eastern half of the United States and not least in Springfield. chandler robbins founded Greenway Academy in 1848, a boys' preparatory school, and it was soon housed in an asymmetrical

---

[6] *A. J. Davis, Downing's associate, was designing Italianates, as was Calvert Vaux, and Gervase Wheeler. Richard Upjohn, another recent émigré English architect, was a strong supporter of the style. In 1845, Edward King of Newport, Rhode Island, had built a villa from an Upjohn design which even Downing had to admit was excellent (fig. 83, pages 64–65). And in England, Prince Albert designed the Italianate Osborne House for Queen Victoria.*

85 *Greenway Academy, 1852*

87 (inset, below). A more elaborate workman's cottage by Downing. 88 (far right, bottom screen). An elaborate cubic Italianate design by Downing. 89a (far right, top). The Christopher Thompson House, South Lowry Avenue, Springfield, Ohio, built 1854, now razed. 89b (bottom, left). The Robert Thorpe House, Old Route 70, Harmony Township, Clark County, Ohio, ca. 1854. 90 (at right). The Riccardi Palace, Florence, Italy. 91 (above). The Vendramini Palace, Venice, Italy.

Italianate, very similar to several of Downing's designs *(fig. 85, previous page)*. Many years later it was remodeled into the Mitchell-Thomas Hospital. It stood on East Main Street, where later would be located the Springfield Builders' Supply Co. The building was razed after the new City Hospital was built in 1903–1905 on Selma Road. Although constructed somewhat later, the Downey House at High and Sycamore Streets greatly resembles Greenway and is also typical of the asymmetrical Italianate with tower *(fig. 86, page 66)*.

Although Downing could be visionary, aesthetic and romantic, he could also be a hardheaded realist when necessary. He was keenly aware that not everyone could afford an Upjohn villa and often spoke about the futility of building great mansions. His books contain many designs of a very plain, utilitarian nature, yet relieved by just enough decoration to make them attractive, but not expensive *(fig. 87, inset at left, in box)*. He also knew that many people preferred squares or rectangles and that these could also contain more useable space than an irregular plan. In his *Architecture of Country Houses*, Downing proposed several designs for homes encompassing all of these points *(fig. 88, screen, far right)*.

The style found great popularity and acceptance in this area and good specimens are still quite common today. The Christopher Thompson House on South Lowry Avenue and the Robert Thorpe (farm) home on Old Route 70 in Harmony Township are two excellent examples *(fig's. 89a, top, right, & 89b, below)*. Both were built about the same time, ca. 1854, and each is of the rectangular box form, but with the low, hipped Italianate roof supported on brackets. Constructed in the transitional period when Greek Revival was still being practiced, both have very similar, classical door surrounds.

While rectangular boxes may be viewed as a purely utilitarian form, it should also be remembered that they are a form that was used in early Renaissance Florence for two especially important buildings, the Strozzi and Riccardi palaces *(fig. 90, above)*. Each of these is a transitional production, having the heavy, rock-faced

89a) The Christopher Thompson House, South Lowry Avenue, Springfield, Ohio, 1854.

masonry and rounded arch openings of the Romanesque, but eaves in the Renaissance style. The triangular pediments on the first-floor window frames of the Riccardi are also in Renaissance style. The upper windows on both of these, as well as the Vendramini Palace in Venice *(fig. 91, far left, top)*, are the undoubted models for the main, ground- floor windows in the Upjohn design. It amounts to a pointed, Gothic window which has been reworked into a rounded opening.

   Here then is an early example of the famous eclecticism which has been so roundly censured in Victorian buildings by many people. Yet, what it actually does is contribute to a building's interest by deleting that which is uninteresting and substituting that which is attractive. Upjohn's open arcades on the first and second floors of the central block can be found in a number of Italian Renaissance palaces; it is particularly noticeable in the sixteenth-century Farnese Palace at Rome ✸ *(fig. 92, right, at top)*. His windows with alternating pediments could have come from any number of different buildings.

Windows, in fact, are distinguishing hallmarks of the different Italianates. Downing seems not to have manifested any particular interest in the rounded arch window; everyone else did. In his last book, *The Architecture of Country Houses*, Downing gave two basic versions of an Italianate window, ✸ *(fig. 93, at right, in box)*. Both of these are rectangular and represent the Renaissance shape, without any of the decorative elements, such as a triangular pediment. The use of the rounded window with tracery by Upjohn swept the country. In Springfield the simple rounded window can be found on innumerable houses, especially in the area directly south of the downtown ✸ *(fig. 94, page 65)*. And the rounded form with Gothic-like tracery can be found on several houses, especially the later home of O. S. Kelly at Fountain and Mulberry *(see fig. 77, pages 60–61)*.

The rectangular or cubic box form of Italianate also found two other important uses. Being symmetrical, it was easily adapted to the Springfield habit of building "double" houses. This symmetry also made it convenient as a commercial building "for corners." One-half of the first floor on the actual corner could be used as a store. The other half, up and down, could be a house. The area above the store could be an apartment, entered from the side or rear. Thus one building could furnish and satisfy three uses ✸ *(fig. 95, at right)*.

Italianate elements could, of course, be extracted from the style proper and applied to another. One of the most frequent borrowings was the open arcade with arched openings which is found in the Upjohn design. Besides the already noted Farnese Palace, it is the main motif of the Library of St. Mark in Venice ✸ *(fig. 96, second inset, far right)*, and the famous Basilica Vicenza in the city of Vicenza, designed by Palladio. These elegant creations in stone were translated to America where, worked and reworked and finally vernacularized by carpenters, they became the simple porches seen on so many Clark County homes of the 1850–1870 period.

Another borrowing was the windows. The O. S. Kelly House is just one of many which, with pitched roofs, are vernacular homes for a northern climate, but which have utilized Italianate windows. One of the most curious adaptations is the Dynes House, just outside of South Vienna. From the four free-standing chimneys and the different brick between the two floors, it appears to have started out life as a Late Federal cottage.

92 (at top). The Farnese Palace, Rome, Italy, 1530–46.
93 (right). An enriched window design, by Downing.
96 (above). Library of St. Mark, Venice, Italy.

95 Commercial building, South Charleston, Ohio.

page 71

Subsequently some alterations were made in the roof and an almost Gothic gable added. Finally the windows and doorways were altered. Probably an earlier door surround was removed, the lower windows narrowed, and Italianate moldings added—semiarched below, full arch in the gable. The brickwork lintels for the earlier windows and doors can plainly be seen ✸ *(fig. 97, bottom)*.

Two other elements of the Italianate style were once extremely important. One of these, the *belvedere*, has completely disappeared and the *campanile* is scarce, found on only a very few homes with a semidetached tower, such as the Downey House and several on North Limestone Street.

As previously noted, Italianate houses have a low, hipped roof. This amounts to saying that they are like a squat pyramid, which has had the upper portion with the point cut off—they are truncated. This created four gently sloping sides with a flat center. A trap door was often placed in the flat center for easy access to the roof. This flat area was usually enclosed with a low, decorative fence, but in more expensive homes there was often a room built here with windows. This was called a *belvedere* and might be purely decorative, but could provide a snug retreat or study.

Such houses were extremely few in Clark County and all seem to have disappeared. The most famous of these was the home of G̃eorge D̃ibert, off South Yellow Springs Street ✸ *(fig. 98, at right)*. We should note that this flat area with only a trapdoor and railing was also common on eighteenth-century Neoclassical style homes. In modern times that area has been called a "Widow's Walk," supposedly built so that the wives of sea captains could scan the horizon for their returning husbands—who often didn't! The notion is apocryphal at best. It was probably designed for easy access to the roof when wooden shingles often caught fire from chimney sparks.

97 (below). *The Dynes House, South Vienna, Ohio.* 98 (at right). *The George Dibert Residence, Atlas of Clark County, Ohio, 1875.* 99 (above). *Florence Cathedral and Campanile (belltower).*

97 *The Dynes House, South Vienna, Ohio.*

The country houses of central and northern Italy frequently retained watchtowers, left from mediaeval times, when it was necessary to keep a lookout for approaching armies. Churches and cathedrals also had such semidetached towers for their bells or baptistery *(fig. 99, inset, far left)*. These towers were gradually lumped together in the architectural vocabulary under the term *campanile*. In pre-Civil War days, American asymmetrical Italianates commonly had these campaniles, more for decoration than anything else. The Downey House and Greenway Academy each had one. However, as a semidetached unit of the structure, it gave little useable space. Architects and builders therefore gradually blended it into the body of the house where it was little more than a gable, or squat tower, at best.

By the beginning of the Civil War in 1861, the Italianate house in America had undergone the majority of its vernacularization and become a standard house form. For practical purposes, Greek Revival was dead and Gothic Revival fading. The Italianate, on the other hand, whether asymmetrical or cubic, had proved a useful form and would remain a durable building style for almost twenty more years. Its versatility was extraordinary.

An Italianate could be built in a most stark fashion with virtually no embellishment, or it could drip with woodwork, some carpenters and ersatz architects striving to outdo each other in devising complicated brackets for the eaves.[7] Yet formalism could still be achieved by using the cubic shape with a central hallway.

On the other hand, the asymmetrical suited the period's preference for two parlors; the better room being to the front and the entrance on the side into the second parlor, or "sitting room," which we would call a family room today. The thousands of these houses that line the streets of Springfield are mute testimony to the popularity of the style *(fig. 100, next page)*.

[7] The terms "Carpenter Gothic" and "Steamboat Gothic" refer to the often fantastically intricate brackets and tracery found on houses and the interiors of steamboats in the period 1850–1870. While having some Gothic elements, they are generally derived from the Italianate style, rather than the Gothic Revival.

98 *The George Dibert Residence, Atlas of Clark County, Ohio, 1875.*

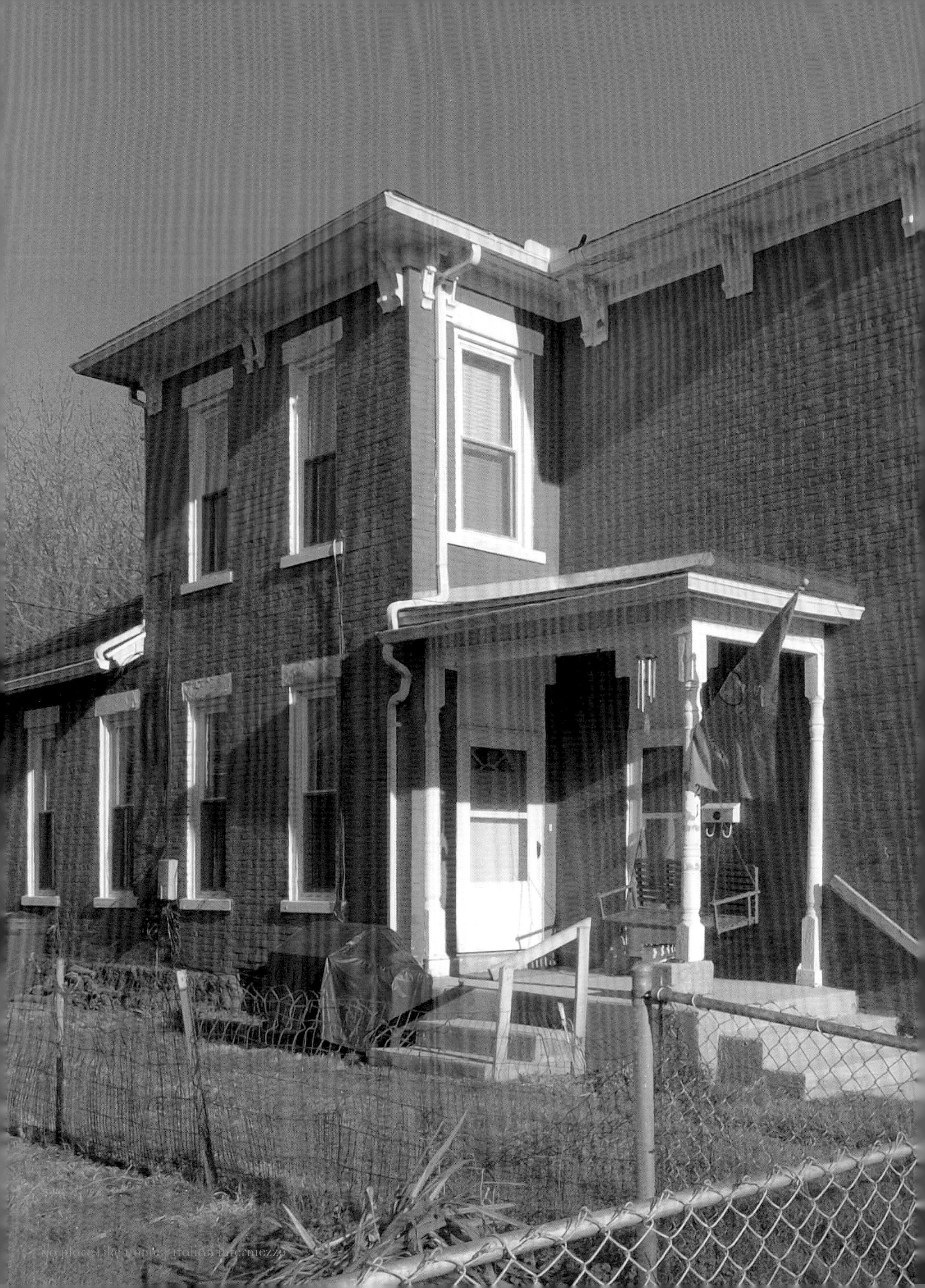

100 *A row of Italianate houses, North Light Street, Springfield, Ohio.*

Remus
GARBLED ITAL

When A. J. Downing discussed architectural designs in Italian modes, he was rather careful to be precise in his choice of words. For him, irregular or asymmetrical designs with towers were "Italian," or "Suburban Italian villas or cottages," depending on the size. The first such major building in the United States was the residence of Methodist Bishop Doane in New Jersey ✽ *(fig. 101, right, top)*. Designed by John Notman, it was simply described by Downing as "...one of the best examples of the Italian style in this country." He followed the same system in describing those of a cubic or rectangular box form. Yet, as early as 1849, he tacitly admitted that some were calling these "Tuscan." He used the term particularly in reference to the many such Italianates being built in New Haven, Connecticut ✽ *(fig. 102, right, at bottom)*.

The term "Tuscan" was derived from that area of north-central Italy—Tuscany—where the style supposedly originated. Their hallmark, of course, was the rounded arch window, which both Notman and Upjohn dearly loved to incorporate into their designs. Downing, however, probably took the wisest course in steering clear of the term. The rural Italian houses in which he took special interest regularly had the rectangular plain windows, which we have mentioned before. It was principally in the towns and cities where the rounded, Romanesque arch was to be seen ✽ *(fig. 103, at left)*.

Modern writers have tended to be less precise and have lumped together just about everything of Italian origin in nineteenth-century architecture under the heading "Tuscan." Not only does this cause confusion, but it is also inaccurate, inasmuch as there were three different modes of Italianate architecture. The first two of these have been previously discussed. The third, the Renaissance style, did not begin to be felt until the later 1850s. Yet it was the Civil War, perhaps more than anything else, that truly prompted its widespread utilization.

101 (top). Residence of Bishop Doane, Burlington, New Jersey; one of earliest Italianates in America, from Downing.
102 (bottom). A generalized design of the "Tuscan" villas being built in New Haven, Connecticut, in the 1840s, from Downing.
103 (at left). An 1864 view of the Italian town of Arpino, where Cicero was born, illustrating the mixed Romanesque and Renaissance elements desired by some architects.

Chapter EIGHT

In 1861, America was a busy nation tottering on the brink of full-blown industrialization. War production in the North pushed the country over the brink and committed it forever to the new form of manufacturing *en masse*. At the same time, it rapidly accelerated a change in the social structure that had begun in the 1850s.

As a democratic republic, the United States, especially in President Jackson's time, had grown to detest any form of aristocracy, whether based on birth, money or politics. But with industrialization, the picture changed. Only a small percentage of the population had the financial means to build and operate factories. These people, not the proprietors of great estates with whole villages upon them, nor the owners of great plantations with hundreds of slaves, came gradually to control the lives of dozens, hundreds, or even thousands of individuals. The wages they paid granted them virtual ownership of the employee, and there were many to take his place from among newly arrived immigrants. Replacements, if needful, were cheap to buy.

These proprietors, or capitalists, increasingly sensing the gulf that separated them from their employees and others, tended to become closed elite and required architecture suitable to its newly found social position. Architects found no difficulty in moving from rural, irregular, or cubic Italianate to urban Italian Renaissance. The changes were relatively minimal and consisted principally in an enriching process. The results, however, were most dramatic.

Although the house might be asymmetrical, it was arranged so that there was a prominent block at the front, the features of which were perfectly symmetrical. The corners were often framed with shallow pilasters, or *quoins,* to create a framework. Within this were the canonical three openings: two windows and a central door on the first floor, and three windows on the second. The whole structure was done, if at all possible, in cut stone, stone veneer, or at least the façade in stone. When stone was not an option, then high-quality brick was required. Frame construction was only a last resort.

The central section with doorway was brought slightly forward and the door recessed within an arched opening, often framed itself with elaborate pilasters *(fig. 104, at top).* If possible, a stone or other portico covered the doorway.

The roof projected heavily, supported on elaborate, scrollwork brackets. The area immediately below the eaves was commonly paneled in wood or metal and pierced for narrow, horizontal attic windows, commonly

104 Design for Renaissance style door cap and surround

STYLE No. 44. Scale 3-8.

106 Renaissance triangular window caps, and a rounded

STYLE No. 46. Scale 3-8.

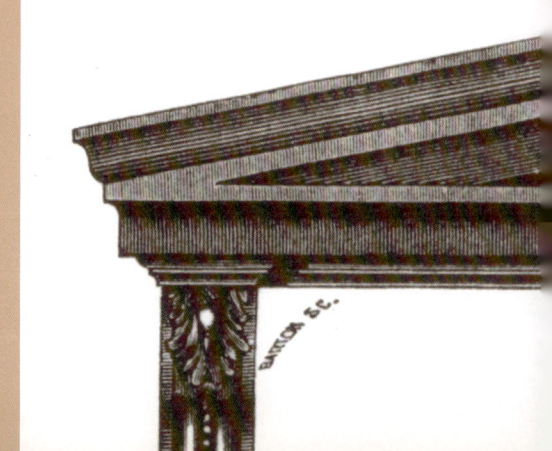

called "eyebrow windows." This paneled area, or *entablature*, was often considerably wider and richer than was customary on the simple Italianate (*fig. 105, background screen*). At the eaves, above the central section, the low, hipped roof rose into a triangular pediment which itself was heavily decorated with moldings.

Windows in these Renaissance houses were highly embellished also, and were usually of two types: those of a slight or "flat" arch design and those of a triangular design, as opposed to the rounded top of the Tuscan mode. These decorative window and door "caps" as they are sometimes called, were often made of stamped sheet iron and painted to resemble stone, so also were door "surrounds" and pilasters (*fig. 106, bottom three panels, left*).

Unlike pre-War days when a wealthy man might live next door to a middle-class or poor man, the wealthy now tended to segregate themselves, building, if at all possible, on a knoll or hill. If that were not possible, then at the very least they tried to construct on double or triple lots to effect separation. The overall impression of these homes was money, power and a formality that was not to be breached. American wealth had come to associate itself with Renaissance princes, if only unconsciously.

The overwhelming power of the exterior of these homes was relieved here and there by carving. Windows were quite susceptible to such, often featuring a keystone in the middle of the top of the framework. Upon this keystone sculpture might be executed, such as monograms or arabesques. Those pilasters which had decorated capitals frequently were done in a softer style than their Renaissance or Classical archetypes. Then, too, purely decorative carvings, such as baskets of fruit, often appeared on porticos and entryways.

Despite these various softening techniques, it was an inescapable conclusion that, for the moment at least, the Romanticism of the period 1840–1860, with willowy, delicate characters, had been shelved. Its place was immediately taken by a sort of sticky, middle-class sentimentalism that doted upon plump children (they obviously did not have consumption!), buxom belles, fluffy kittens and faithful dogs. The era of aesthetic thought and romantic reflection was definitely "out." America was soon to be surfeited with a diet of happy, well-fed industrialists, and their families.

Despite what may be said about the social values of the 1870s, and the personages attached to them, it is inescapable that the building of a Renaissance house in nineteenth-century America required men of an extraordinarily skilled nature. Contractors had to have workmen who could execute fine stonework and superlative carpentry and their like is scarcely to be found today.

page 79

The John Foos House, 810 East High Street.

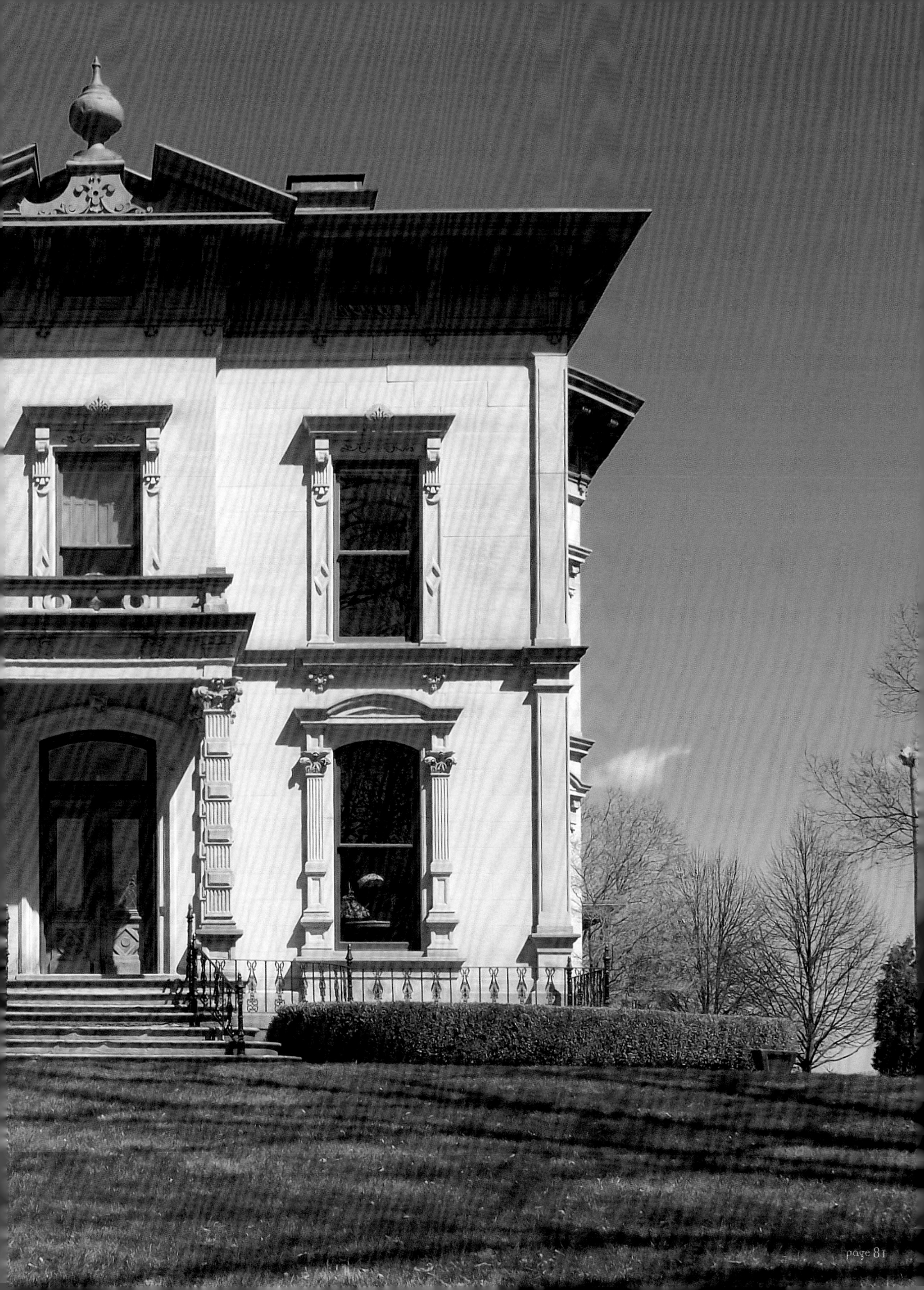

111 *The Bateman-Wildman House, 59 S. Chillicothe St., South Charleston, Ohio, 1874.*

fig. 112

107 (far right). *The Rinehart-Bowman House, 815 East High Street, Springfield, built 1870–73.* 109 (screen, at left). *Design for a Renaissance house with Tuscan windows and vernacular porch, by S.B. Reed, House Plans for Everybody, 1876–78, edition of 1882.* 110 (bottom, right). *The John P. Winters House, 133 W. High Street. Winters was one of the owners of the Transcript Printing Co., built ca. 1869–70.* 111 (top). *The Bateman-Wildman House, 59 S. Chillicothe St., South Charleston, Ohio, built for Henry Bateman in 1874.* 112 (bottom, left). *The Penfield House, Spring and Pleasant Streets, Springfield, Ohio, ca. 1875, now razed.*

no place like home | garbled italian

Springfield is fortunate to possess two outstanding Renaissance houses, the Rinehart-Bowman and the John Foos on East High Street which are the equal of anything built elsewhere in the United States. The former of these required about three years to complete, 1870–1873, and the latter about five years, 1870–1875 ✺ *(fig's. 107, bottom, right & 108, previous page).*

JOHN W. RINEHART, who built the one, rose from humble beginnings to end as one of the partners in the Rinehart-Ballard Co., which manufactured threshing machines known nationally. John Foos, likewise, rose from humble beginnings to become a major financial figure in Springfield, owning, among other interests, the St. John Sewing Machine Co. and the Cottage Color Paint Co. Both men were proud of their success and let the world know it through their homes.

Houses in the Renaissance style were not, however, an exclusive privilege of the wealthy. Families of middle- and upper-middle-class status quickly found that architects were pouring out pattern books containing Renaissance designs for moderate purses ✺ *(fig. 109, screen, far left).* These were usually in frame construction, but many fine examples in brick exist. In more rural areas, retiring farmers, like the *nouveaux riches* in cities, adopted the style and fashion set by industrialists and manufacturers. Many Midwestern towns have whole streets lined with these spacious homes, built by the sons of those pioneers who arrived about 1800 and were now retiring. An outstanding example was the John P. Winters House on West High Street, now razed ✺ *(fig. 110, left, bottom).*

South Charleston has several excellent examples, including the homes of the late Virginia Robinson and that of Mr. and Mrs. Austin Wildman ✺ *(fig. 111, at top).* Of these two, the Wildman House is the purer, chaster design, dating to 1874. The Robinson House is an extremely fine example of a "Carpenter" Renaissance. Herein a local contractor-carpenter has tried to duplicate in wood all the details normally found in brick or stone. A similar structure, the Penfield House, now demolished, once stood at Spring and Pleasant Streets in Springfield ✺ *(fig. 112, left, bottom).*

fig. 110

fig. 107

page 83

America,
MORE GARBLED

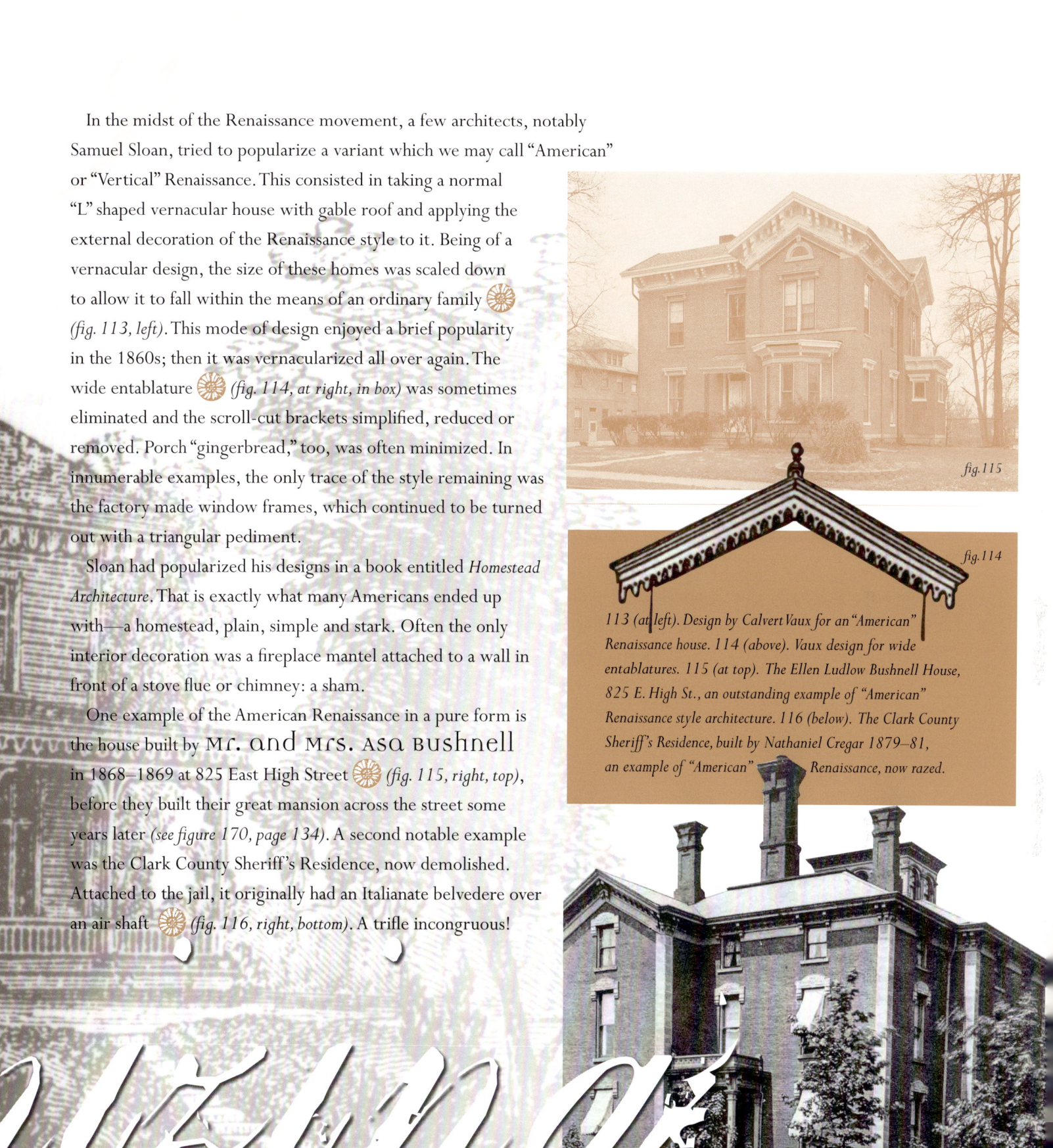

In the midst of the Renaissance movement, a few architects, notably Samuel Sloan, tried to popularize a variant which we may call "American" or "Vertical" Renaissance. This consisted in taking a normal "L" shaped vernacular house with gable roof and applying the external decoration of the Renaissance style to it. Being of a vernacular design, the size of these homes was scaled down to allow it to fall within the means of an ordinary family *(fig. 113, left)*. This mode of design enjoyed a brief popularity in the 1860s; then it was vernacularized all over again. The wide entablature *(fig. 114, at right, in box)* was sometimes eliminated and the scroll-cut brackets simplified, reduced or removed. Porch "gingerbread," too, was often minimized. In innumerable examples, the only trace of the style remaining was the factory made window frames, which continued to be turned out with a triangular pediment.

Sloan had popularized his designs in a book entitled *Homestead Architecture*. That is exactly what many Americans ended up with—a homestead, plain, simple and stark. Often the only interior decoration was a fireplace mantel attached to a wall in front of a stove flue or chimney: a sham.

One example of the American Renaissance in a pure form is the house built by Mr. and Mrs. Asa Bushnell in 1868–1869 at 825 East High Street *(fig. 115, right, top)*, before they built their great mansion across the street some years later *(see figure 170, page 134)*. A second notable example was the Clark County Sheriff's Residence, now demolished. Attached to the jail, it originally had an Italianate belvedere over an air shaft *(fig. 116, right, bottom)*. A trifle incongruous!

fig. 115

fig. 114

113 *(at left). Design by Calvert Vaux for an "American" Renaissance house.* 114 *(above). Vaux design for wide entablatures.* 115 *(at top). The Ellen Ludlow Bushnell House, 825 E. High St., an outstanding example of "American" Renaissance style architecture.* 116 *(below). The Clark County Sheriff's Residence, built by Nathaniel Cregar 1879–81, an example of "American" Renaissance, now razed.*

fig. 116

Going ITALIAN

Chapter NINE

One very prominent development during the Renaissance period in eastern cities is almost completely lacking in Springfield—the Brownstone Row house. In some places such as New York, there were erected whole blocks and neighborhoods of narrow town houses with adjacent/party walls. They were faced, or veneered, with a chocolate-colored stone quarried in Connecticut. The "Brownstone" has been the subject of countless books, novels, plays and movies, and is always shown as a run-down apartment house or slum dwelling.

In reality, these structures began their existence as good-to-elegant residences for one family each, plus servants. Springfield had only two specimens that approached the Brownstone in form. One of these was a line of brick row houses which once stood where the Huntington National Bank is now located, on the south side of North Street in the first block west of Fountain Avenue. The other was another series of brick row houses built on West Mulberry Street between 1860 and 1870. Set on a high foundation, they resembled the eastern prototype that was reached by a flight of stairs. Their highly carved window and door lintels also mark them as unusual ❈ *(fig. 117, top, right)*. This type of lintel or "dripstone" as it is also called, is sometimes given the name "inchworm" type and is a cross between the rounded and rectangular forms ❈ *(fig. 118, below)*. Multiple-frame ❈ *(fig. 119, bottom)* row houses, however, were not uncommon in Springfield. The best example of these ❈ *(fig. 120, at right),* on East Main Street, was unfortunately demolished some years ago.

The purest form of Italian Renaissance was, at best, a short-lived style locally and did not survive the 1870s; the same is true of American Renaissance. Both of these styles

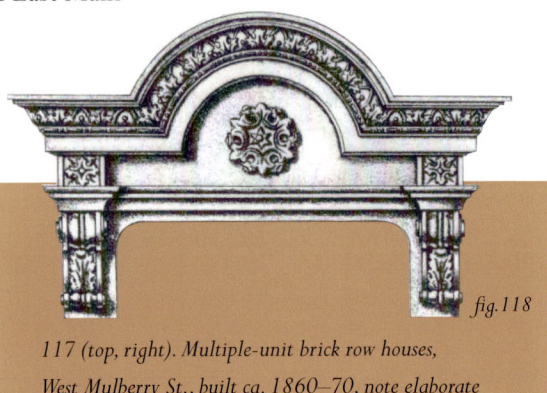

117 *Multiple unit brick row houses, West Mulberry St., ca. 1860–70.*

fig.118

117 (top, right). Multiple-unit brick row houses, West Mulberry St., built ca. 1860–70, note elaborate "dripstones" over windows, now razed. 118 (above). "Inchworm" type window cap, from the Philadelphia Architectural Iron Co. catalog, 1872. 119 (below). Multiple-unit row house design by S. B. Reed, 1878. 120 (at right). Frame double house, East Main Street, now razed.

fig.119

contributed immensely to architecture by providing a rich source for borrowings, for this was the era of wholesale *eclecticism*. Again, it was window styles in particular that were borrowed. True, as well as derivative, Renaissance windows were placed on all manner of houses, even the Gothic (fig's. 121a & b, next pages). Commonly made of stamped sheet iron, a house could be "modernized" by nailing these new lintels over the old ones. In virtually no time, the old Gothic or Greek Revival house could become a smart, up-to-date residence, just as houses today are remodeled by the addition of vinyl/aluminum siding and "replacement" windows.

By the mid-1870s, the stone lintels that were used on more expensive homes had undergone a change that resulted in a virtually uniform type that can be seen all over Springfield and Clark County. Architects and designers combined the rounded Italianate Tuscan with the pedimented Renaissance. What emerged was one with a flat top, small triangular point and two perpendicular sidepieces that dropped a short distance down the sides of the window. By the end of the decade, the small point on the cross member had been eliminated.

The era being one of marvelous, inventive genius, machines were soon designed to produce standardized carving in the middle of the cross member of the lintel or "dripstone."

120 Frame double house, East Main Street, now razed.

In many instances older Italianates were remodeled with the new style of lintel. Where the owner did not want the expense of new masonry work, he could, as we have remarked, use new, prefabricated sheet metal lintels that could be affixed over the old ones. The Harbaugh-Rice House at Pleasant and Center Streets was a simple, cubic Italianate in the 1850s. In the 1870s, after a little nailing and careful painting, it became a "new" house in the current style ✺ *(fig. 122, above)*. It was razed in 1977.

The triangular pediment over the central section also underwent considerable metamorphosis. It was bent and twisted into a variety of shapes, some reminiscent of bonnets or nuns' veils. In time it gradually shrank until, by the 1880s, it was often little more than a hood over a window high above the doorway ✺ *(fig. 123, page 91)*.

The process of listing Renaissance forms, their mutations and redeployment in houses of other styles, together with earlier forms, could be prolonged *ad infinitum*. So great was the eclecticism of the period, that some houses literally defy categorization. Perhaps the best summation is to present a picture of the house built by industrialist P. P. Mast about 1880–1881. Mast lived in this house while his old home across the street was being razed and a new mansion erected for him. The new house would eventually become part of the Knights of Pythias Home.

This structure, which we can call Mast's second home ✺ *(fig. 124, right)*, is basically an irregular, hipped-roof Italianate. Yet, consider the multiplicity of architectural details that embellish it, most of which are derived from Renaissance forms. But this complicated image is only part of the story of the 1860s and 1870s.

We should be aware that the Italian Renaissance image in architecture was not derived necessarily directly from Italy. As early as 1855, the French Emperor Napoleon III had begun his program of the restoration and enrichment of Paris. Part of this program was the completion of the Louvre, which had been begun in Renaissance style in the sixteenth century. Another major project was the construction of the Paris Opera House ✺ *(fig. 125, above)*. The Louvre presented a building already partially completed in an earlier age and it was necessary only to follow

no place like home | more garbled italian

121b *Renaissance details, Center and Clark Streets.*

121a (above). *Gothic Revival House with Italianate windows, North Limestone Street, now razed.* 121b (at left). *Renaissance details grafted onto an 1850s house at Center and Clark Streets, now razed.* 122 (far left, at top). *The Harbaugh-Rice House, Pleasant and Center Streets; another house with 1870s details added to an 1850s structure, now razed.*
124 (above, top). *Residence of P. P. Mast, 910 W. High Street, built 1880–81. Note complexity of details, including arcading to right of entry porch, and miniscule triangular element in second floor window hood. This was Mast's second home.*
125 (far left). *The Paris Opera House, by Charles Garnier (note: home of The Phantom of the Opera!).*

page 89

123 (at right). The J. Warren Keifer House, East High Street, from the 1875 atlas, later the site of Catholic Central High School.
126a (at top). The former Woods-Algier Funeral Home, North Limestone Street, ca. 1860–70.
126b (screen, below). The Phillip Weimer House, 648 East High Street, as it appeared in the 1875 Atlas of Clark County, 1875.
126c (above). Residence at Wittenberg and North Streets, built by Nathaniel Kinsman, Superintendent of the Springfield Gas Works, ca. 1875.

the previous stylistics. The Paris Opera House by Charles Garnier, while akin to the "Berlin School" of monumental architecture, was largely Garnier's own invention and, when asked what was its style, he replied, "Napoleon III!"

Both of these structures were erected when Americans were first beginning to study architecture at the *Ecole des Beaux-Arts* in Paris, Richard Morris Hunt and Henry Hobson Richardson being two of the more outstanding. Hunt, particularly, but many others, too, helped to bring back to America and popularize the open arcading, classical pediments, and other of the motifs of the Italian Renaissance, which were being revived in Paris. The rounded top pediments, particularly of Garnier, gradually filtered down to the local scene and we can hear faint echoes of them in such buildings as the former Woods-Algier Funeral Home *(fig. 126a, left)*, the Weimer House on East High Street *(fig. 126b, below)*, the John P. Winters House (now razed) on West High Street *(see figure 110, page 83)*, and the Kinsman House at Wittenberg and North Streets *(fig. 126c, left)*.

In matters of architecture, the United States had maintained continuity with England, from the foundation of the country until about 1860. In other areas, however, France had been the style setter, dictating fashions in furniture, clothing, and *objets d'art* since the time of Napoleon I. The only sphere where French influence had not penetrated was architecture. With the resurgence of a strong political power under the Emperor Louis Napoleon, it was inevitable that Gallic fashion would invade this realm, too. Yet this was only the beginning. France had merely helped in the transition to the Renaissance style; it would soon supply in wholesale a new mode, the Second Empire or Mansard style. But England would eventually retaliate!

123 *The J. Warren Keifer House, East High Street.*

Phineas P. Mast's West End

In that massive work, *The Biographical Record of Clark County, Ohio*, the anonymous author includes a portrait of P. P. Mast standing in his library consulting a thick reference book. Clad in a neat suit with high, standing collar, Mast is the very paradigm of the careful, calculating businessman. Whoever the photographer, he assuredly understood his subject and captured his essence. Mast seems to have done everything in life as a series of careful calculations, only one of which was ever flawed.

Phineas P. Mast was born January 3, 1825 in Lancaster County, Pennsylvania. Of his youth little is known, other than that he was raised on a farm—but so was 90 percent of the American population at that time. His family migrated to Ohio in 1830, where they settled in the Urbana area. He had four brothers and three sisters. What we do know is that he graduated from Ohio Wesleyan University in 1849 and married one Anna M. Kirkpatrick on his twenty-fifth birthday, January 3, 1850. They had no children, but Mast would later adopt the three daughters of his deceased brother, Isaac.

Mast stayed on the family farm until 1856; he was learning the *business* of farming, as well as trading grain and produce. Then, as did so many of his contemporaries, he came to Springfield in 1856. This was the last boom year before the Panic of 1857.

Knowing all aspects of the farming business, Mast was now ready to enter the regular business world and make money out of his background, certainly more than if he had remained a simple farmer. He quickly went into a partnership with John H. Thomas. The new firm, Thomas & Mast, manufactured agricultural implements and was able to withstand the Depression of 1857. In 1871–1872, Mast bought out Thomas's interest in the firm, which then became the P. P. Mast & Co.

It was at this point that Mast, the calculator, made his only mistake in life. Deciding for some reason that he did not care to live on either the developing South Fountain Avenue or East High Street, Mast decided to develop West High Street. In this he may have been encouraged by Rev. Charles Stroud, who also lived in the area. Mast would build and occupy three successive homes on West High Street (*see figures 124, page 89, & 171a, page 130*).

In 1869, Mast and other investors created the Citizens Street Railway Co. and bought the old Pennsylvania House and land. A large barn, which had once housed drovers' animals, now housed the horses and mules that pulled the six cars along the rails. The following year, 1870, he created The Mast Foos Co., at the west end of the line. By 1878 the railway was in receivership and up for a sheriff's sale. Mast bought the street railway, which serviced his area, as well as his *quondam* partners' interests. He now ran the railroad by himself and leased out the Pennsylvania House for other purposes. Although Mast Foos would prosper, his new neighborhood never developed beyond a district of workingmen's homes, clustered around his stone mansion on a knoll on West High Street.

In 1877, the P. P. Mast & Co. had acquired a Louisville, Kentucky, agricultural publication. Two years later a new firm, Mast, Crowell & Kirkpatrick, was established to publish the magazine under the name of *Farm and Fireside*. J. S. Crowell, a dynamic editor from Louisville, became its manager and made it the most widely read agricultural journal in the United States. The editor was Mast's nephew, T. J. Kirkpatrick, and Mast himself supplied the financial backing.

Unwilling to leave "any bases uncovered," Mast also created the P. P. Mast Buggy Co. and was involved with the Second National Bank until his death. As was the case with other prominent manufacturers and businessmen in Springfield, he was a well-known contributor and supporter of his own church, as well as others. He also served as mayor for two years.

There was only one wrong calculation in his life, but that cost him dearly. He could not create his "shining city on a hill," only a castle on a knoll, without friends and associates. Perhaps the most unkind cut of all was that his adopted daughter, Belle, moved to East High Street. Daughter Florence did not survive him, and daughter Elizabeth was frequently absent from the house at West High Street and Western Avenue. There would be no Mast dynasty to love and maintain the house in the West End, much less promote the neighborhood.

The first of three residences P. P. Mast built on W. High St. was featured in the 1875 Atlas of Clark County. At far left, Phineas P. Mast, pictured in his library. He lived in lonely splendor on Springfield's west end while other scions of Springfield society were happily ensconced on East High St. and South Fountain Ave.

page 93

Mansar
FRENCH CURVES

In 1849, Louis Napoleon Bonaparte was elected President of France, succeeding the bumbling Louis Philippe, King of the French, who had abdicated during the Revolution of 1848. Three years later, after something of a *coup d'etat*, Bonaparte was proclaimed Emperor of the French. The glory of France was about to be resurrected.

Louis Napoleon *(fig. 127, below)* was the son and only surviving child of Napoleon I's brother Louis. He, in turn, had married Hortense, the daughter of Napoleon's first wife, Josephine, by her first husband, Eugene Beauharnais. That made Josephine both sister-in-law and mother-in-law to Louis. Never mind, no blood lines were crossed.

Louis and Hortense were miserable from the start and separated after a few years. Their son had a melancholy childhood and the gloom never completely left his personality. Yet, what he lacked in personal magnetism was compensated by his delightfully intricate and scheming mind. As early as 1836, he had tried a Castro-like invasion of Strasbourg, but completely failed, as he did again in 1840. But now that he had won, he was about to return glory to the Bonaparte name. If he could not attract and hold people through charisma like his famous uncle, there were other ways.

Napoleon III, to use his impartial title, had one enduring project which seemed to override all others, the enrichment of Paris, which Napoleon I had never had time to complete. Soon after his enthronement, Napoleon III hired the Prussian engineer Baron Georges Haussman to begin the modernization of the city. Haussman, in turn, worked for the next twelve years to eradicate mediaeval Paris *(fig. 128, right, top)* with its tottering buildings and narrow, tortuous streets, the setting of several famous stories by Poe, such as *Murders in the Rue Morgue*. Haussman's greatest creations were the magnificent boulevards, which are the hallmark of the city today *(fig. 129, right, bottom)*. The boulevards also made guerrilla fighting, features of the 1830 and 1848 revolutions, almost impossible!

127 (immediate left). Woodcut portrait of Emperor Napoleon III; Harper's Monthly, 1853. 128 (above). Woodcut view of mediaeval Paris, Harper's, March, 1853. 129 (below). Woodcut view of modern Paris, Harper's, March, 1853. 131 (at far left). Spelling book illustration of a Mansard house under construction, 1872.

Chapter TEN

While the Baron was demolishing houses and creating streets, others were building or restoring. Not only were cathedrals rescued from the ravages of the Revolution of 1789, but also the Tuileries Palace was refurbished, the Louvre completed, and the Paris Opera House constructed. Yet, it was the boulevards that came to influence America, since these were soon uniformly lined with new apartment buildings. These structures almost uniformly adopted a form of roof, invented in the seventeenth century by the architect Mansart. This style of roof was built in two sections. The first part rises from the eaves at a steep angle. At about two-thirds the final height, the roof angle abruptly changes to a very shallow one. Thus the rook has two sections, each with its own angle. The lower section was often roofed with slates, but wooden shingles—especially ones with fancy cut edges—were often substituted in America. The upper portion was almost invariably done in some sheet metal covering.

These roofs, called *mansard* after anglicizing, usually had the lower portion shaped in either a concave or convex curve. Often, too, dormers protruded from the lower portion and extended out to the eaves line. Such dormers were regularly fitted with scroll-cut side panels and finials for extra embellishment. Sometimes in the early 1870s and 1880s, the lower roof profile was that of a simple straight line, after the fashion of French chateau roofs.

Napoleon III and his wife, Eugenie, had visited the first world's fair at the Crystal Palace in London in 1851 and immediately recognized the value of such extravaganzas for propaganda purposes. In 1855 and then again in 1867, two further such fairs were held, but this time in Paris. Even today, some old firms still reproduce on their labels the medals they won at those two exhibitions. Visiting foreigners, especially democratic Americans, were immediately entranced by Napoleon's brilliant court and the new Paris he was creating. Rococo furniture and furnishings, with sinuous curves ❋ *(fig. 130, far right)*, became ever more popular and architects were soon creating "French style" houses in every part of the United States ❋ *(fig. 131, page 94)*. Perhaps the most famous, if only a movie set, was the great mansion created on the barren plains of Texas in the movie *Giant*.

Producing a "French style" house was in no way difficult, nor was it novel. Robert Morris, the financier of the American Revolution, had built a mansard-roofed mansion in Philadelphia before 1800 ❋ *(fig. 132, at right, top)*. The architect he employed was the same Major L'Enfant who laid out Washington, D.C. Unfortunately for Morris, the architect was

132 Robert Morris's mansion, Philadelphia; 1853.

133a Mansard design, architect George Woodward, 1865.

133b Another Mansard design by Woodward, 1867.

extravagant and the final cost sent him into bankruptcy.

Since the mansard roof had been developed at the end of the Renaissance, it was entirely appropriate to graft one of these roofs onto the body of the then popular Renaissance Revival house-type. From there it was but a short step to using almost any form of Italianate architecture—cubic or asymmetrical—for the bulk of the structure ❧ *(fig's. 133a & b, at left)*. In time, about the only house style that did not receive a mansard was the Greek Revival and that was only because the roof in the Greek style was an integral part of the design and could not be separated.

For many years the whole era of the mansard roof has often been called "The General Grant style." This is due to the fact that a number of government buildings were erected in Washington during Grant's Presidency, in this French mode. Grant's poor reputation as President and his unfortunate, but accidental association with some shady financiers have caused the style to fall into disrepute. For this reason, modern architecture historians prefer to call it the Mansardic or Second Empire style, conveniently forgetting Grant altogether!

The variety of mansard-roofed buildings in America is nearly endless. Almost anything could and did receive one—from outdoor privies to the Executive Office Building in Washington. The style seemed suited to almost any location. Yet it was basically a tall vertical style that looked best along city streets, or in areas with tall shade trees. Only when a farmer or rancher erected one on the prairies of Kansas or Texas did the style seem out of place—and then it looked ridiculous ❧ *(fig. 134, background screen)*! The great point was that it was "modern" and "elegant." It did not matter that the roof design was 200 years old and the interior furnishings

fig. 130

130 (above). Spelling book illustration of typical Second Empire parlor with Rococo furnishings, 1872. 132 (left, top). Robert Morris's mansion, Philadelphia; artist's reconstruction for Gleason's Pictorial Drawing Room Companion, August 6, 1853. 133a (left, middle). Design for a Mansard house, by architect George Woodward, 1865. 133b (left, bottom). Another design for a Mansard, by Woodward, 1867. 134 (background screen). Mansard in a rural setting. Spelling book illustration, 1872.

no place like home | french curves

136a The E.C. Middleton / William Warder House, as it appeared in 1889.

136b The same house today.

page 99

fig. 135

were imitating those of a century before. The major requisite was to copy the elegance and opulence of Paris and Napoleon's court. Their refinements were mirrored, if a trifle blurred, in large amounts of machine-cut wooden decoration that dripped from the eaves and dormers of American homes. Not all Mansard houses were overdone, however.

In Springfield, the Second Empire style never found wide acceptance and was thus confined to a few commercial buildings and a handful of houses. While all of the commercial structures that had such have disappeared, most of the houses are still standing. Probably the earliest and most visible of the commercial Mansards was the famous Black's Opera House at the corner of Main and Fountain, which was gutted by fire in 1903. It had been completed in 1869.

Perhaps one of the earliest homes in the Second Empire style was that built by one Dr. Samuel E. Adams, on the southeast corner of Dayton Road and Isabella Street, on the far west side of the city (*fig. 135, top*). Dr. Adams advertised himself as an "electropathist" and later as "Homeopathic and Electrical Physician and Surgeon." The house has a mansard roof, but is in other respects an utterly plain cubic Italianate with vernacular porch. It is thus only a tentative stab at the style. Yet it is quite large and spacious, and probably served the needs of the doctor's "electropathic institute" quite well. Since electropathy was a fraud, no doubt the remote location of the doctor's residence was an asset.

Beginning in the late 1860s, and peaking in the mid 1870s, there was a "rash" of Mansards constructed in the two fashionable areas of town. Elijah C. Middleton built an elegant and very chaste home on East High Street at Lincoln Avenue in 1868 (*fig's. 136a & b, previous page*). The external ornamentation was restrained and he went so far as to copy the French style of inserting stone quoins in the corners of his brick walls. His creation was, perhaps, the most elegant mansion ever created in Springfield. About the turn of the twentieth century, the house was heavily remodeled, losing its original architectural integrity. For many years it was owned by William Warder of the Warder & Barnett Flour Mills. Today it houses the Jones-Kenney-Zechman Funeral Home.

no place like home | french curves

135 *(inset, top, left). Residence built by Dr. Samuel Adams at 35 Dayton Avenue, ca. 1870.*
137a *(above). The Francis M. Bookwalter House, as it appeared in Springfield Illustrated, 1889.*

The Francis Bookwalter House today.

That year of 1875 saw Francis Bookwalter erect one of the two truly pretentious Second Empire homes constructed in Springfield, the other being by Benjamin Warder. The former, built of frame, its three floors, slate roofing, iron cresting and other embellishments cost Bookwalter $19,000 to erect. The Bookwalter House has so many embellishments, in fact, that it is the virtual paradigm of what a "High Victorian" house is supposed to be. Originally it had only a small portico over the front steps *(fig. 137a, previous page)*, but sometime after 1889 the porch was lengthened to cover the entire front *(fig. 137b, at left)*. In addition, within the twentieth century an underground garage was excavated under part of the building. In recent years restoration work has been initiated on the house, in keeping with its position in the South Fountain Avenue Historical District.

The following year, 1876, Bookwalter's brother-in-law, Warren C. Leffel, built another Mansard diagonally across the street, at the corner of Fountain and Miller. Like Bookwalter's, Leffel's home is also built of frame construction *(fig. 138a, page 106)*. This house is much closer to the typical home in that style and is a virtual duplicate of one shown in Bicknell's 1871 *Village Builder and Supplement* book of house designs. This particular contribution to the book was designed by D. B. Provoost of Elizabeth, New Jersey *(fig. 138b, page 106)*. The body of the house has the appropriate Renaissance window caps and the dormers are enriched with scroll-saw-cut side panels. The gingerbread turnings, brackets and latticework on the front porch, however, are not original to the house and probably date to the late 1880s, or early 1890s.

The cost of erecting a Second Empire mansion appears to have varied greatly. Lewis C. Huffman retired from farming in 1875 and moved into Springfield, where he built a fine brick house on South Limestone. That house *(fig. 139a, page 107)* cost him $7,000 to build, considerably less, proportionately, than Bookwalter's cost. The latter, however, had ornamented his with extensive exterior woodwork and interior fittings, which must have driven up the price. A quick glance will show that Huffman's house is only a slight degree more elaborate a house than Dr. Adams'. Both have the same design of roof and porch. It is the richer window caps that mark the only real difference between the two, indicating perhaps that the same builder constructed both.

The last and greatest of the Mansards was built by Benjamin H. Warder *(fig. 139b, next page)* on a tract of land he owned along Lagonda Avenue, facing St. Bernard's Church. This twenty-room brick mansion and its numerous outbuildings is said to have cost more than

page 103

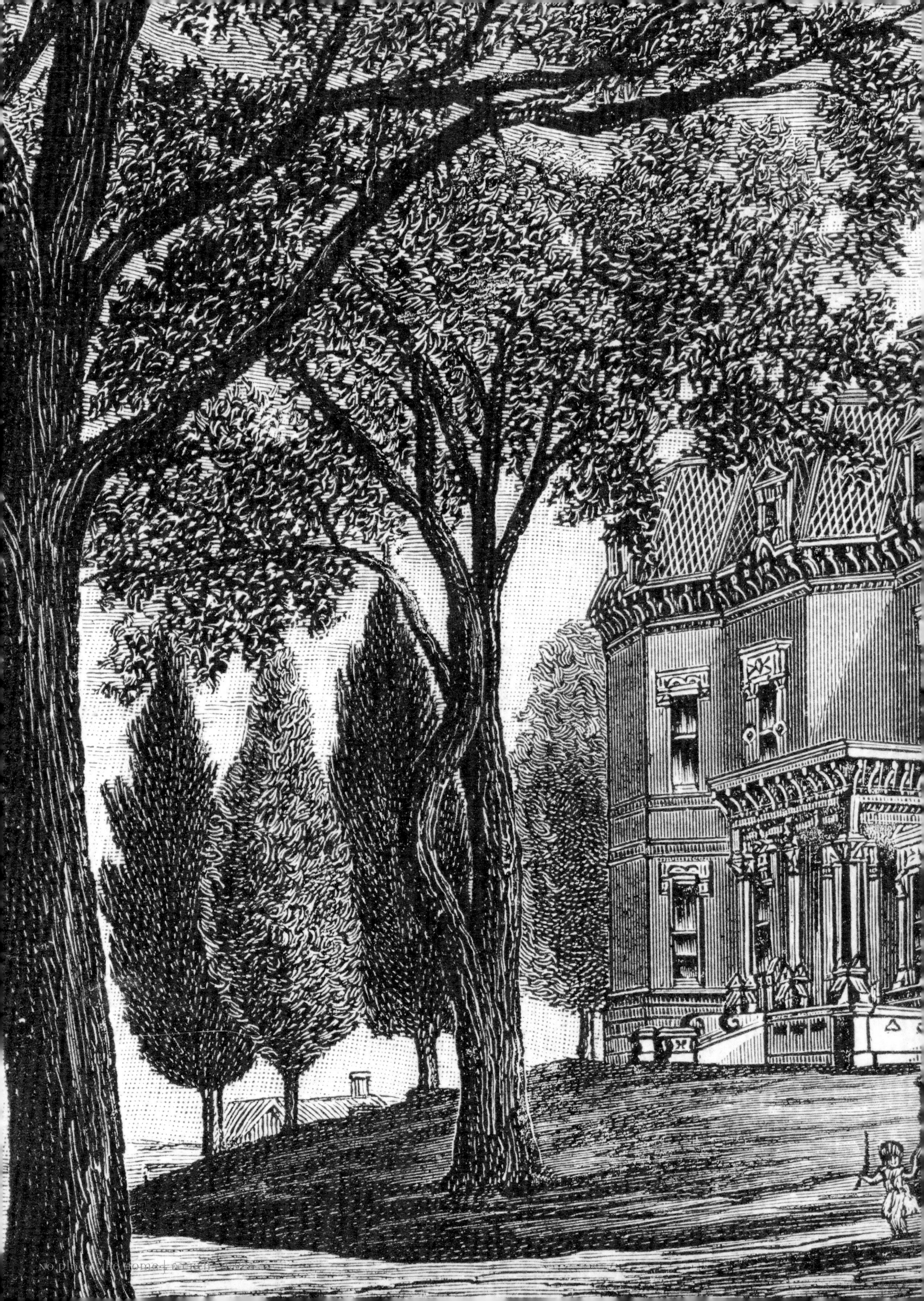

139b The Benjamin H. Warder house, Lagonda Avenue, the last of the great Springfield mansards.

no place like home | french curves

fig.138a

fig.138b

$100,000 when it was built in 1876–1877. The Warders enjoyed it only briefly, for they moved to Washington, D.C., in 1883 and there they had a new mansion built by the noted architect, H. H. Richardson. The house in Springfield eventually fell on bad days and sold for a mere $5,000 a few years before it was demolished in 1939.

Although there were a few other Mansards in town, including the 1870 home of Jerome Fassler, William Whiteley's original partner, they have all disappeared. Sometime after 1882, W. C. Downey made an addition to the rear of his home at High and Sycamore, which was done with a mansard roof (fig. 140, at bottom), but this marks the extreme end of the style in Springfield.

Americans usually remember Napoleon III today only as a man whose intrigues placed an Austrian, Archduke Maximillian, on the throne of Mexico, in 1864. This caused the United States to worry through the end of the Civil War that a second front would open. In June of 1867, Maximillian was finally overthrown and executed by the followers of Benito Juarez, played in a memorable movie by Paul Muni. The end had begun for the French emperor.

By July 1870, the wily Otto von Bismarck, Chancellor of Prussia, had maneuvered France and his country into a war. The Germans were said to have better road maps of France than the French, and the conflict lasted only one and one-half months; Napoleon III capitulated to Prussia on September 1, 1870. He was held prisoner until March of the following year, when he was released and went into exile in England. There he died of a kidney disease on January 9, 1873.

During the Emperor's brief imprisonment, the Parisian Communists had temporarily established a commune and run riot. The Tuileries Palace was burned, as was the Hotel de Ville (City Hall) and the great Vendome Column pulled down—a monument to Napoleon I. The Prussians besieged the city and blockaded it completely, while shelling the public buildings. The only visitors were carrier pigeons, and the populace was finally forced to eat sewer rats. Only then did they surrender. The Empire was finished for a second time and a new Republic proclaimed. With the death of Napoleon's son in 1879, there were no further immediate Bonapartes to claim the throne. For the eastern United States, the brilliant life and architectural style of Imperial France began to die almost as soon as Napoleon III surrendered at Sedan. For Springfield it took a little longer for *rigor mortis* to develop.

fig. 139a

138b (at left). Design for a Mansard house by D. B. Provoost, of Elizabeth, New Jersey. The design appeared in The Village Builder and Supplement by the A. J. Bicknell Co., New York, ca. 1873. This is clearly the same design used for the Warren Leffel House, 138a (inset, left), built 1876. 139a (above). The Lewis Huffman House, 411 South Limestone Street, built ca. 1876. 140 (below). The W. C. Downey House, 736 E. High St., rear addition, ca. 1882.

fig. 140

South Fountain Avenue

The period of the early 1850s was an era of expansion and growth. In Springfield there was the almost weekly creation of new businesses and factories. While James Demint had platted blocks and lots to the west, much of the east and south still had large areas of undivided land. The east side was slower to develop, perhaps due to the terrain being a high ridge. The National Road, entering town on East Main Street, apparently was of little help in populating this area. The only other major entrance was along East High Street, also known as the Chillicothe Road, and that brought in only the occasional farmer.

The area now called South Fountain Avenue, then Market Street, experienced two major periods of growth in the nineteenth century. Both of these appear to be the result of expansion due to industrial and commercial growth.

The first *Directory of the City of Springfield* in 1852 had a map appended to it. This map shows South Market Street running from the downtown Market Square to approximately Miller Street. The street is divided into blocks on the west side, by the intersections of Washington, Jefferson, Mulberry, and South/Pleasant Streets. On the east side there were no divisions, or intersections below Washington Street. In 1853 there were one hundred and twenty-five lots added to this area by John Kenny, John Patton, and Letitia Eaker

Of these subdividers, two are shown in the 1852 *Directory* to have been "carpenters," and lived in the south end of Springfield. Letitia Eaker, whose name is misspelled in the Rockel's *History* as "Baker," apparently lived in Dayton. According to the 1860 U. S. Census, she was the head of her household—no husband—and had real estate worth $120,000 as well as personal property in the amount of $50,000. This was a very wealthy woman for 1860. No doubt much of it was derived from South Fountain Avenue land holdings, and even more would be made in the next decade as her lots were sold off to eager buyers.

The inevitable conclusion is that both men, Kenny and Patton, being of the same occupation, probably knew each other, especially since the two lived so close together. The fact that the lots are sequential in numbering and situation only heightens the impression that these two are small contractors who had bought the land earlier in the belief that it would appreciate in time. Perhaps they even went so far as to build some housing on their lots "on speculation." Letitia Eaker, however, is a mystery, worthy of a movie, but the plot of which will have to be explored another day.

no place like home | french curves

Historically the major entrance to the city from earliest days had been on the south side. With the establishment of a new Market Square and proper City Hall on Market Street in 1848, the impetus was provided for new growth to the south.

By 1865 and the end of the Civil War, the demand for farm machinery had grown to an enormous degree. This was due to the War's demands for food and the opening of the Western wheat fields. Agricultural implement manufacturers were doing a huge business. Whiteley, Fassler & Kelly had done so well that they had built an immense factory on the east side of the Market Square and running for an entire block between High and Washington Streets. This, too, in addition to all of the downtown businesses and railroads, was a spur for additional residential growth to the south.

In 1865 Jacob Huben, listed in the 1852 *Directory* as a brewer, added a number of lots on both South Limestone and Market Streets. He was followed by William Houck, a well-known brick maker, who joined with gunsmith Peter Slack in 1867 and added a large chunk of lots on the west side of Market between Kizer and Obenchain. Interestingly, like the earlier developers, Houck and Huben lived approximately across the street from each other, Houck on the east side of Limestone, south of Pleasant, and Huben on the west side.

With these post-Civil War additions, most of South Fountain, or Market Street, was broken into house lots and available for building. The street perhaps reached its apogee in the later 1870s with the construction of the Second Empire homes of Francis Bookwalter and his brother-in-law, Warren Leffel (*see fig's 137a, page 101, & 138a, page 106*). Both were officers of the James Leffel Company, only a few blocks directly north. Many other prominent Springfielders, such as Theodore Troupe, Cyrus Kissell and his son Harry, would also build homes on the street, in every style from Italianate to Queen Anne.

By the 1920s, however, demographics would change and residents would resettle in newer neighborhoods, such as Ridgewood. It was only East High Street that would hold out against residential trends for a longer period of time.

A row of houses in the National Register District of South Fountain Avenue (also see overleaf).

no place like home | french curves

page 111

Eastlake
OLDE ENGLISH

No period of nineteenth-century architecture is free from the overlapping of several styles. While one mode is at its zenith, another is fighting for survival and still a third is either aborting or dying. This situation is particularly true from 1870 onward. A rapidly increasing population of natives and immigrants fostered the need for extensive building. The need was met by great quantities of factory-produced elements plus the adoption of nailed-together balloon-frame construction, which greatly simplifies the basic structural work on houses. At the same time, increasing contacts with European culture tended to stimulate the desire for architectural change—or at least, for alternative styles.

When Louis Napoleon became Emperor of the French in 1853, the cubic/rectangular Italianate had become the popular style, although a few die-hards continued to build Greek Revival for a while and Gothic Revival would never be completely forgotten. The beauty of the Italianate was that it was extremely adaptable. As the French influence grew, Italianates quickly became the more formal Renaissance styles by the addition of a small pediment and a few columns at the front doorway. Those who wished to be up-to-date in their architectural taste could easily add or replace the low hipped-type roof with a high mansard type. Both Mansard and Renaissance styles coexisted throughout the 1850s and 1860s for those of means. For the ordinary family, a plain Italianate continued to be the architectural "workhorse" until about 1880.

141 (above). Louis XIV sofa from Downing's Architecture, 1850. 142 (left, below). Building in the Eastlake style, erected by the State of Ohio at the Centennial Exhibition at Philadelphia, 1876. This structure is one of the few from that Exhibition still standing in Fairmount Park. It was built from twenty-two varieties of Ohio sandstone. 143 (below). Design for a rural, English-type farmhouse; by Downing, 1850. 145 (far left). Stick-Eastlake residence of W. A. Scott, 806 South Fountain Avenue.

Chapter ELEVEN

During the period of French styles in architecture, the Court at Fontainebleau also dominated the realm of taste in furniture. Initially the Empress Eugenie had dictated a taste for Rococo furniture, by her preference for a revival of the style of Louis XIV. These were pieces that were all curves: cabriole legs; round, oval or "turtle-top" tables, and balloon-, shield- or medallion-back chairs *(fig. 141, previous page)*. Her taste later shifted to Louis XVI, which had more rectilinear lines and legs that were straight with turnings. The surfaces of these pieces were regularly covered with decorative overlays on veneer—especially those of a swirling grain which would be laid on/in the top of the frame which would be of a straight grain pattern. While Louis XIV furniture was commonly made of mahogany or rosewood (real or imitation), Louis XVI was the era of walnut. In expensive pieces, all manner of inlays were used, from mother-of-pearl to exotic, imported woods.

A sharp reaction to these elaborate, revival styles began with the publication in London, in 1868, of Charles Locke Eastlake's *Hints on Household Taste*. Although Eastlake was an architect, his book was principally concerned with furniture. Like later architects, such as Frank Lloyd Wright, he believed in "honest" furniture. For him this meant a return to a highly rectangular style, largely devoid of ornamentation with the exception of incised lines and circular, trefoil or quatrefoil cut-outs. In short, it was a simplified combination of Mediaeval and Gothic. A chronological sequence of important events at this time is worth consulting:

1868 Eastlake first publishes his book;
1870 Napoleon III surrenders to the Prussians;
1872 Eastlake's book is republished in Boston.

By 1876 "Eastlake style" houses began to appear everywhere in the United States *(fig. 142, previous page)*. Eastlake himself did not like the American adaptations of his work and repudiated any connection with them, yet his stylistics persisted in American homes into the 1880s and in furniture into the 1890s. The basic concept of the "Eastlake" house was neither difficult nor novel. Given the 'hint' that English Gothic was the desirable medium, architects simply opened their pattern books and began drawing on what Downing, Wheeler and others had been advocating since the 1850s *(fig. 143, previous page)*. To the basic Gothic Revival house they added furniture details as advocated by Eastlake, interpreted architecturally and modified by them.

The "Eastlake" house, like the Gothic Revival, was an asymmetrical

148 *Eastlake residence, 563 S. Limestone Street.*

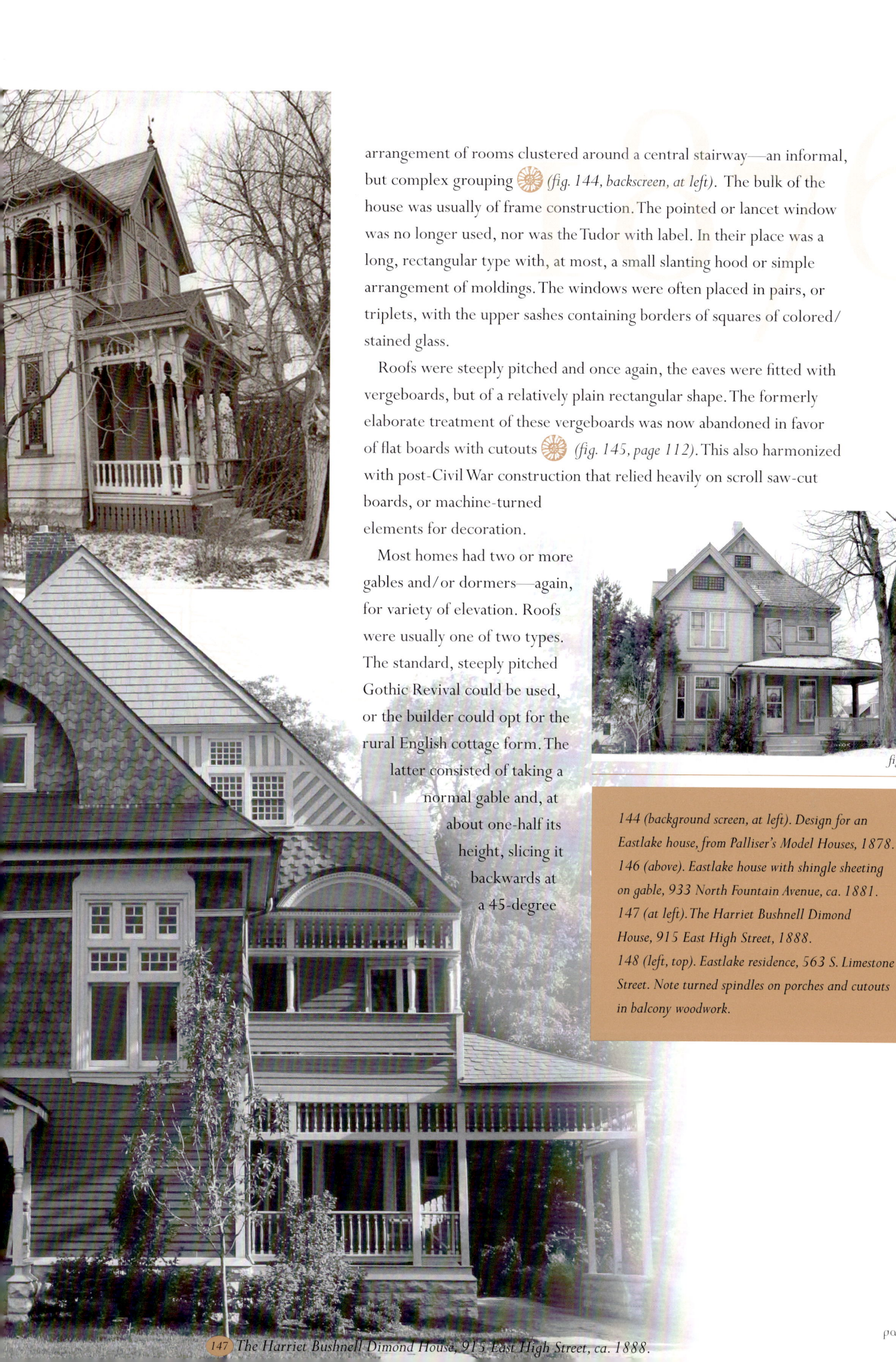

arrangement of rooms clustered around a central stairway—an informal, but complex grouping *(fig. 144, backscreen, at left)*. The bulk of the house was usually of frame construction. The pointed or lancet window was no longer used, nor was the Tudor with label. In their place was a long, rectangular type with, at most, a small slanting hood or simple arrangement of moldings. The windows were often placed in pairs, or triplets, with the upper sashes containing borders of squares of colored/stained glass.

Roofs were steeply pitched and once again, the eaves were fitted with vergeboards, but of a relatively plain rectangular shape. The formerly elaborate treatment of these vergeboards was now abandoned in favor of flat boards with cutouts *(fig. 145, page 112)*. This also harmonized with post-Civil War construction that relied heavily on scroll saw-cut boards, or machine-turned elements for decoration.

Most homes had two or more gables and/or dormers—again, for variety of elevation. Roofs were usually one of two types. The standard, steeply pitched Gothic Revival could be used, or the builder could opt for the rural English cottage form. The latter consisted of taking a normal gable and, at about one-half its height, slicing it backwards at a 45-degree

fig. 146

144 (background screen, at left). Design for an Eastlake house, from Palliser's Model Houses, 1878.
146 (above). Eastlake house with shingle sheeting on gable, 933 North Fountain Avenue, ca. 1881.
147 (at left). The Harriet Bushnell Dimond House, 915 East High Street, 1888.
148 (left, top). Eastlake residence, 563 S. Limestone Street. Note turned spindles on porches and cutouts in balcony woodwork.

147 The Harriet Bushnell Dimond House, 915 East High Street, ca. 1888.

page 115

angle, producing what is called a *truncated*, or *jerkinheaded* gable *(see figure 143, page 113)*. This form, while never wildly popular, was used well into the twentieth century on a number of different types of structures, especially urban carriage houses, and later garages. In both types of gable, the exterior surfaces were routinely sheathed in wooden shingles ✺ *(fig. 146, previous page)*.

On a few homes, the shingling was extended to cover additional portions of the structure. The Dimond House at 915 East High Street ✺ *(fig. 147, previous page)* is such a structure. Due to recent restoration efforts, the shingles are once again highly visible. They and the extensive surfaces they cover make a brilliant contrast to the otherwise routine Eastlake turnings of the exterior decorative woodwork. The effect, then, was picturesque, providing a pleasant contrast to the balance of the house and its other siding. Whether this habit was derived from traditional New England construction, Dutch designs or furniture veneering is impossible to say. It probably contributed to the development of Richardson's Shingle style of architecture.

It was the front porch of the Eastlake house that received some of the most dramatic treatments. They were now extended across the entire front of the house, with the area under the eaves of the porch being filled with what we today particularly call gingerbread. Here the scroll saw found its greatest employment, being used to create a variety of designs. The most popular of these were the trefoil and quatrefoil, or three- and four-lobed openings. A number of other designs were also used, such as intersecting "S's" and circles ✺ *(fig. 148, previous page)*. The supporting posts, as well as the spindles in the railings, were machine turned on gang-lathes and

fig. 149

149 (at top). The Potter-Troupe House, 724 South Fountain Avenue. Note the lacy cutout work in the porch gable.
151 (inset, above). Farmhouse design, "in the Swiss manner," Downing, 1850.
156 (right). The Rowley-Bosart House, 845 East High Street, 1884.

156 *The Rowley-Bosart House, 845 East High Street, 1884.*

looked very much like contemporary chair and table legs. Even today, occasionally, an antique table will be found which, upon examination, will be found to have been homemade, using such spindles for legs.

A second area that soon underwent special treatment was the intersection of vergeboards. Architects found that a pleasant treatment was created by filling this pediment area with designs in the Eastlake style such as sunbursts and fanlights, done in incised lines. Another method was to use cutouts and thereby create a lacy effect ✹ (fig. 149, page 116).

The habit of drawing on the early English domestic style of architecture gradually led to the adoption of one prominent feature—the overhang. In the Mediaeval house the second story usually projected or overhung the first floor by several feet. This characteristic was quickly introduced into many Eastlake houses, particularly in the form of projecting second-story bays which were boldly marked by an elaborate but nonsupporting bracket with sunburst or rosette motif ✹ (fig. 150, below). The device and motif were also used on window hoods and porch pediments. The overhang also found expression in ever-deepening eaves, which created a general projection over the entire house.

Downing and his contemporaries were all very much impressed with the functionalism and appropriateness of the Swiss chalet house form, particularly the more unsophisticated types. Downing crossed this concept ✹ (fig. 151, page 116) with the Gothic trusses of Mediaeval English buildings and created an exposed framework pattern for gables. These latter left much of the timber framing for eaves and gables bare and exposed to view. Architects revitalized the idea in the 1870s and 1880s, but now often as a purely decorative pattern and it is sometimes seen on houses of other than Eastlake stylistics. For lack of a better name, this has come to be called the Stick style ✹ (fig. 152, background screen, at right).

The Eastlake movement appears to have gotten off to a slow start in Springfield. Men of wealth and means, such as the Fooses and Warders, were still building in the Renaissance and Mansard styles in the mid-to-late 1870s. This conservative bias was also seen in the new Jail and Sheriff's Residence of 1879, which was done in an outmoded Italo-American Renaissance style. On the

fig. 150

153 *South Charleston Depot, 1878–79.*

154 *The Weigand House, 812 Center Street, post-1870.*

NO PLACE LIKE HOME | OLDE ENGLISH

other hand, the little newly built frame depot in South Charleston for the recently constructed Springfield, Jackson & Pomeroy Railroad was utterly *au current* with jerkin-head gable and Stick style eaves (*fig. 153, immediate left*) in 1879. But the average Springfielder continued to create his home in the old-fashioned asymmetrical Italianate style until about 1880.

fig. 155

The area south of Pleasant Street offered a large tract on sparsely settled land. And it was here that much of the early Eastlake-type construction took place between 1870 and 1880. Although heavy use and constant remodeling makes it almost impossible to pick one house as the *first* Eastlake in the area, some early ones can be noted.

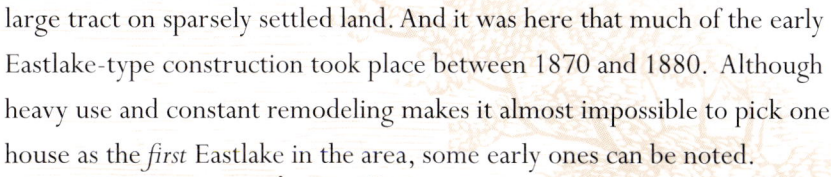

About 1870, G. Weigand began construction of a house at 812 Center Street, which was not finished for several years (*fig. 154, left, bottom*). The porch eaves with their lunettes and quatrefoils, the rectangular vergeboards and the rosettes in the gables all contribute to make this a paradigm of the style. The imitation half-timbering over the second floor windows is an added distinction and hallmark of the style.

At about the same time as Weigand's construction, one G. W. Cogswell took an older Italianate at 520 South Wittenberg Avenue and modeled it into a quasi-Eastlake. The lack of surface ornamentation marks it as an early venture, at best. The small portico, however, with its intricate cutouts in the entablature is characteristic of the style (*fig. 155, top*). This may be just a fragment of a porch that originally extended across the entire front of the house.

The masterpiece of all Eastlake homes in Springfield, formerly owned by the late Helen Bosart Morgan, was built in 1884 by Charles Rowley at 845 East High Street (*fig. 156, page 117*). Perhaps its most outstanding quality is the unity of its design. The porch is, in every respect, perfect Eastlake, with its turned posts, quatrefoil cutouts and pediment with imitation half-timbering framed by simple vergeboards. The filled gables, fitted with double and triplet windows, also fit the style perfectly. Even the roof cresting, finials and articulated chimneys come from the best pattern books. Perhaps the cleverest, yet subtle, device is the surface decoration between the second- and third-floor windows. Not only does it add interest to the surface and break the pattern of the siding, but it also leads the eye upward to the third story. In short, the Morgan House

150 (far left). Eastlake House on North Limestone Street. Note the strongly marked second-floor overhang. 153 (middle, top). South Charleston Depot, Stick style with struts under the eaves; built 1878–79. 154 (immediate left). The Weigand House, 812 Center Street, post-1870. 155 (at top). The Cogswell House, 520 South Wittenberg Avenue, post-1870, now razed. 152 (background screen). Design for a farmhouse with struts in the gables, by Gervase Wheeler, 1853.

158 *The M.A. Hayward House, 901 South Fountain Avenue, ca. 1875–82.*

offers about the best that the Eastlake style had to offer and is to be found in Springfield.[8]

Of only slightly less interest is the house at 821 South Limestone Street ✲ *(fig. 157, right)*, built sometime between 1875 and 1882. Its chief interest centers on the main gable. Here, at small expense to the builder, was created a minor fantasy in woodwork by the use of a three-level arrangement. The deep eaves set off by the triangular brackets create the effect of a Swiss chalet and Stick style construction, which are highlighted by the angled sheathing and framing behind on the surface of the house *(see also figure 151, page 116)*. Its size marks it as a modest home, but it certainly was not uninspired.

The M. A. Hayward House at Fountain and Liberty was also built between 1875 and 1882. This home, however, is not so noticeable for inspiration as for discipline ✲ *(fig. 158, at left)*. Surface decoration is kept at a minimum—only a little lacy cutout work at the gables and relatively simple porches with corner brackets in a sunburst design. The sought-after effect is that of quiet, somber dignity and the Gothic Revival body of the house suits the purpose admirably. The corner overhangs and window hoods are not only exemplary of the style, but fit the quiet, retired atmosphere of the structure. The only bit of whimsy attached to the dwelling is the somewhat Chinese porch railing at the first-floor level.

After 1880, the erection of several public buildings, including the new, or second, courthouse and a few mansions in the new style, provided the necessary spark for construction. The location of several major agricultural implement companies within the city also provided the economic incentive to build. By 1889, when *Springfield Illustrated* was published, it was possible to place a respectable number of Eastlake homes within its pages, and lots all over town were being filled with new houses.

With the demise of the French Emperor, empire, and Mansards in the 1870s, the United States had gravitated back into the arms of England and all of its old ties. Although the highest and wealthiest levels of society would always maintain associations with France, their influence would be minimal, especially in ordinary, domestic architecture. Eastlake, however, was only the first step in the re-Anglicizing process.

157 (above). Residence at 821 South Limestone Street, ca. 1875–82.
158 (left). The M. A. Hayward House, 901 South Fountain Avenue, ca. 1875–82.

[8] *Now, at the time of revision in 2007, multicolor paint schemes are returning and this makes the surface decoration of a typical Eastlake infinitely more interesting than it had been for nearly a century.*

Charles Cregar

Of the various individuals who have affected Springfield, few had the impact of architect Charles Cregar. And yet, little enough is known of the man, and no photograph of him survives in any archive. He is a man "known by his works."

Charles Cregar's grandfather, Daniel Creagar (they would drop the "a" in Springfield days), is said to have been born in Germany and died in Maryland. In 1825, during his American career, Daniel Creagar was in Washington County, Pennsylvania, where his son Nathan was born. During the family's years in Maryland, Nathan is said to have studied architecture with Samuel Sloan.

Samuel Sloan was one of the brilliant stars in the American firmament of nineteenth-century architects. Although it was late in his career that he began to use the title "architect" instead of "carpenter" or "builder," nevertheless, his influence was profound. Literally thousands of homes, from grand to insignificant, were constructed across America from his published designs in the period 1850–1870. Although precise documentation is lacking, many homes in Springfield from the later 1860s bear a distinct Sloan imprint. These were the days when Nathan Creagar was acting as a contractor/house builder.

As with so many people in the 1850s, Springfield became a mecca for those seeking new opportunities. Nathan Creagar arrived sometime after 1852 and here, in 1858, his son, Charles, was born. At the time, his father was listing himself in city directories simply as a carpenter.

Charles Cregar, according to the only printed biography of any length, had the usual schooling. However, he did attend and graduate from the Springfield High School, which was slightly unusual in that era for someone of the Blue Collar Class. Either he or his father had plans for his future.

Following his graduation from high school, Cregar began studying draftsmanship. Eventually he would move to Ft. Wayne, Indiana, where he would do an eighteen-month work study with a prominent draftsman, T. J. Tolan.

Returning to Springfield, he went to work as a draftsman for the T. B. Peet Co., which made galvanized fixtures. By 1879 he had progressed enough in his career that he married. At the same time he landed the job of superintendent of construction on the new post office building at High and Spring Streets.

In 1883, Charles Cregar became a partner with his father in an architectural office. The following year he decided to open his own business and rented office space in the Mitchell Building, downtown. In 1885 Nathan Cregar would die, after several years of failing health, leaving Charles on his own.

Charles Cregar would design the plans for Springfield's major buildings, including St. Raphael and St. Joseph Catholic Church, St. John's Lutheran Church, Third Presbyterian Church (Northminster), Second Lutheran Church, United Presbyterian Church, Central High School, the Arcade Hotel and, most important of all, the new City Building (now the Heritage Center).

The majority of Cregar's buildings have been demolished over the years, but those that survive are probably his best work, the several

churches, the City Building, and his own home (*see figure 168b, page 128*).

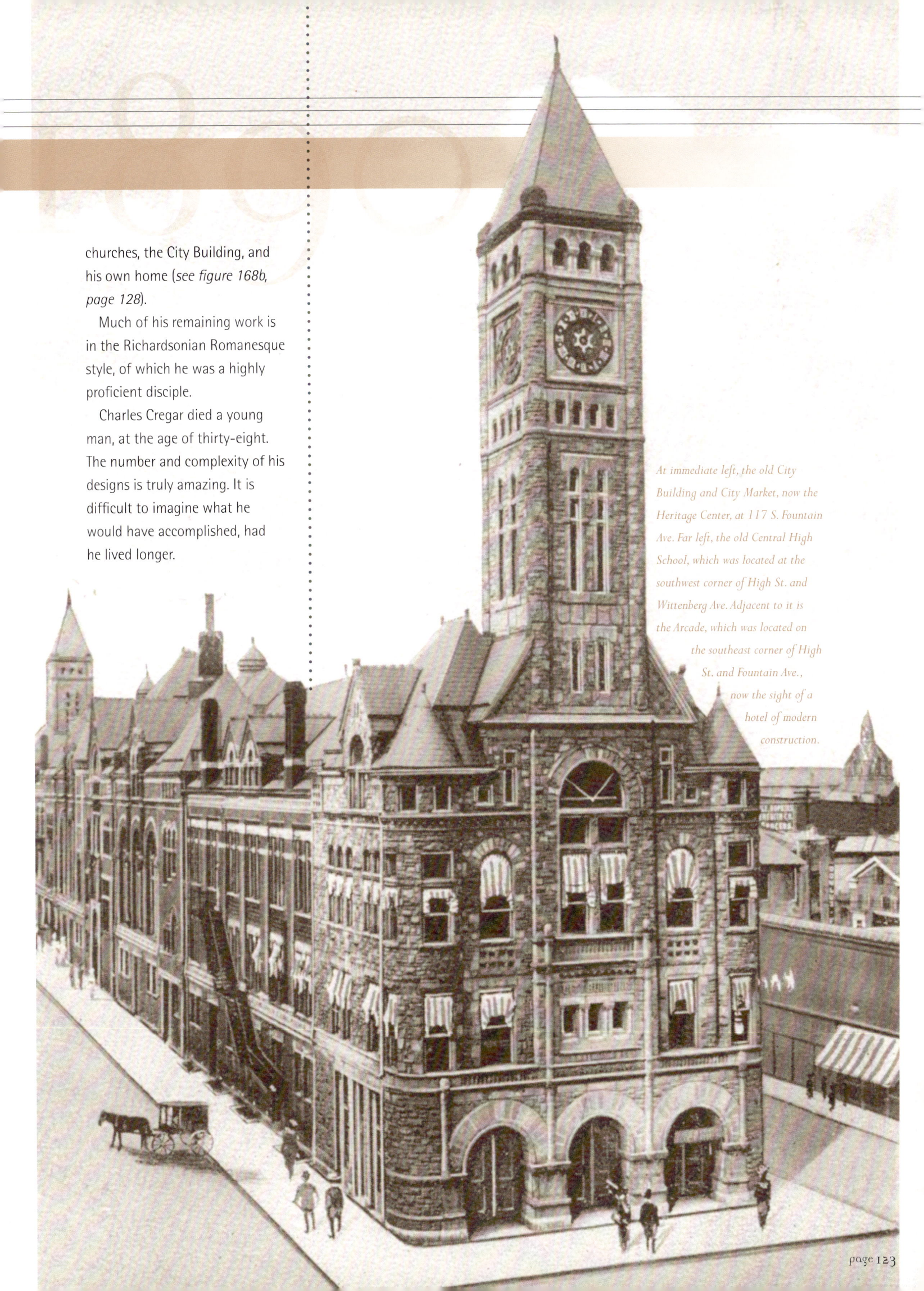

Much of his remaining work is in the Richardsonian Romanesque style, of which he was a highly proficient disciple.

Charles Cregar died a young man, at the age of thirty-eight. The number and complexity of his designs is truly amazing. It is difficult to imagine what he would have accomplished, had he lived longer.

At immediate left, the old City Building and City Market, now the Heritage Center, at 117 S. Fountain Ave. Far left, the old Central High School, which was located at the southwest corner of High St. and Wittenberg Ave. Adjacent to it is the Arcade, which was located on the southeast corner of High St. and Fountain Ave., now the sight of a hotel of modern construction.

Queen An

WHAT'S IN A

The memorable quotation below from Shakespeare, as to the validity or true substance of names, applies to nothing more surely than later nineteenth-century architecture. Until the 1870s few people associated the name Eastlake with architecture, only with furniture *(fig. 159, near left)*. From about 1880 onward, the prevailing style of architecture was known, then and now, as "Queen Anne." It encompassed everything. Today, however, we have subdivided the period and have Eastlake and Queen Anne, as well as Stick style, not to mention Romanesque, Richardsonian Romanesque and Shingle style. Yet, it is not all a muddle of names; there are relationships and progressions.

It has become something of an academic question as to which came first, Eastlake or Queen Anne. Given both the stylistics and antecedents, Eastlake definitely appears to be the first breakaway from the Italian and French styles, with Stick style a variant or offshoot. Both have their roots in the Gothic Revival period. While "Eastlake" has some validity, if only marginal, "Queen Anne" has none at all.

Great Britain's Queen Anne, the last of the Jacobite monarchs, ruled from 1702–1714. It was her reign that saw the popularization of Classical Revival architecture, which would come to be called "Georgian," after the names of three of her successors, Kings George I, II & III. The nineteenth-century style named after her depends almost exclusively on domestic home designs of a more Mediaeval character, as found in the time of Queen Elizabeth I and King James I. Thus, some modern scholars prefer to call this mode after the Royal Family of the seventeenth century, and have renamed it "Neo-Jacobean."

The Queen Anne style was first popularized by British architect Richard Norman Shaw, who began practicing in 1862. Like Eastlake, his works became popular in America in the 1870s. But, it was not until the 1880s, especially in areas removed from the Atlantic seaboard, that his designs began to have a dominant effect on American architecture. Shaw's early designs for homes of modest proportions brought him

161 (far left). Eastlake house at 160 W. College Avenue. 159 (near left). An Eastlake chair, used in the second Clark County Court House, 1881 and thereafter. 164 (above). Old woodcut of Glamis Castle, Scotland. 160 (below). Scotland Yard Buildings, by Richard Norman Shaw.

NAME?

Chapter TWELVE

quick recognition, but it was his later work, especially the Scotland Yard Building (1890) that secured his fame and fixed the general shape of the Queen Anne house ✹ *(fig. 160, previous page)*.

   No matter which name one prefers, the essence of the style is that it is an elaborated Eastlake, with one or two emphasized features. Perhaps the most visible and characteristic of these is the tower. While the Eastlake homes followed the earlier Italian and French styles in occasionally adding a semidetached tower to the bulk of the house, these were generally square or rectangular, with steeply pitched chateau roofs ✹ *(fig. 161, previous page)*. Queen Anne architects, however, fell back on the rounded tower with conical roof. This was nothing terribly new. A. J. Downing was designing houses with rounded, "Norman" towers in the 1850s ✹ *(fig. 162a, page 128)*. Whether architects utilized Downing, or followed a more archaeological investigation, the effect was the same. From the mid- 1880s onward, every

fig.165c

162b Residence with rounded porch and tower, 800 South Fountain Avenue.

house that could afford one was built with a rounded tower or turret on one corner. If wealth allowed, the tower motif was repeated on one corner of the standard wide, front porch, then more picturesquely called a *veranda* or *piazza* (fig. 162b, far left, bottom). Occasionally a hexagonal or octangular shape would be substituted for the round ✦ (fig. 163, above). No matter what the shape, the tower/turret motif was derived from Mediaeval sources ✦ (fig. 164, page 125).

A second prominent characteristic of the style was the continuing elaboration in surface treatment. The average Eastlake house had but two exterior coverings. The lower floors were done in narrow, horizontal siding; while the gables were sheathed in shingles. The random or occasional applied half-timbering now became standard. Other gables had latticework affixed to the surface and still others received factory-made classical swags, garlands and medallions, in addition to dentil moldings. This last was the major concession to the true classicism of the real Queen Anne period. The simple Eastlake siding gave place to a combination effect. The foundations might be high ones of cut stone; next, the first floor of red brick, then the second in horizontal siding or clapboard and finally the gables in shingles or other material ✦ (fig's. 165a, near left; 165b, page 129; and 165c, at left, top).

On the front porch, the cutout gingerbread was gradually displaced by turned work composed of factory-produced spindles and posts, of one form or another ✦ (fig. 166, next page). Vergeboards with cutouts were also eliminated in favor of solid ones with, at most, a scalloped or wavy

---

162b (at left). Residence with rounded porch and tower, 800 South Fountain Avenue.
163 (at top). Residence with octagonal tower, 758 N. Limestone Street. 165a (immediately above). Residence at 833 North Fountain Avenue. This was a transitional structure as the semicircular bay-tower does not dominate the house. Now razed. 165c (left, top). Residence at 309 N. Plum Street. Note the variety of surface treatments. The future of this structure is uncertain.

edge. During the Centennial Exposition of 1876, much interest was taken in the Japanese exhibit, especially their architecture. Soon thereafter houses began to have porches and balconies ornamented with latticework, in imitation of oriental designs (fig. 167, far right, bottom).

One other concession to the true Queen Anne classicism was the employment of Palladian windows—two smaller rectangular windows on either side of a taller, arched one. The style was named after the Renaissance architect, Andrea Palladio. Windows, otherwise, continued rather plain, but often grouped in twos, and the amount of stained glass used continued to rise (fig's. 168a & b, below).

Brick homes did not allow nearly the same facility for decorative embellishment as the frame, except in the gables, cornices and eaves. Yet, where they lacked in turned, wooden decoration, they compensated by the extensive use of cut stone as decorative "belting" or dividing courses, and around windows. John Ruskin, the English art critic, had advocated a style of architecture he called "Venetian Gothic" and which employed polychrome patterns in brickwork. Springfield, except for a faint echo in Recitation Hall at Wittenberg, is largely lacking in this style. Yet occasionally one finds a home of the period with a little polychrome work around the main front window (see figure 168a, inset, below) such as the now razed Charles Phelps House on Ferncliff Place. The architect Charles Cregar accomplished this in his own home by the use of stone dressing around the windows (see figure 168b, at left).

Upon this scene of frenzied searching for a quasi-Mediaeval house form—with creature comforts never known by the Middle Ages—there burst a new name: H. H. Richardson. Richardson was the son of a wealthy Louisiana family, who had been sent to Paris to study architecture, before the Civil War erupted. He remained there at the *Ecole des Beaux-Arts*, until 1865 when, with the family ruined by the war, it was necessary to return home. In 1867 he opened an office with Charles Gambrill. The following year he built his own home, which was merely a hybrid cross between a house with a Queen Anne body and a mansard roof. Until 1872 his work was fairly conventional and only hinted at what was to come.

162a (background screen). "Norman" style residence by the architect West, of Cincinnati, 1850. *166 (above).* Residence at 1019 South Limestone Street. Note elaborate porch post turnings. *168a (inset, at bottom).* The Charles Phelps House, Ferncliff Place, now razed. *168b (below).* The Charles Cregar House, 483 Park Place. This is the only private house proven to be created by Cregar. Note his characteristic sawtooth design in the second floor windows surround.

fig. 165b

fig. 167

165b (above). Queen Anne at its most classical, 815 N. Limestone Street. 167 (left). Residence at Center and Grand Streets; note the latticework arch in the upper porch.

page 129

171a *The P. P. Mast House, 901 West High Street, built in 1882–83 in an attempt to create a new, stylish neighborhood in the west end of Springfield.*

In 1872 Richardson was awarded the commission for Trinity Church, Boston *(fig. 169, at right)*. Now for the first time he displayed the full range of his talents and personal ideas. Part of the curriculum at the *Ecole* was an extremely strict and archaeological study of the previous eras of architecture; e.g., Greek, Roman, Romanesque and Renaissance. The rationale of this curriculum was to train architects to think, by demonstrating how previous ages had solved various architectural problems. For some students this training was a useful servant; for others, a handy crutch. In Richardson's case, the distinction at times becomes hazy. He had become highly enamored of the Romanesque architecture of southern France. That is the essence of Trinity Church. Needless to say, he molded and shaped his historic models to develop his own personal touch and style. Yet, no matter how it is appraised, the fact is that Richardson's use of Romanesque architecture soon swept the nation, and not only did he receive numerous commissions until his death in 1886, but so also did a host of his imitators.

While it is difficult to assemble for a short entry an all-encompassing critique of Richardson's style, a few characteristics may be noted. Above all else, there is a striving for unity of design in his products; a harmonizing of one part with another, and balance. His designs were almost exclusively built in cut stone with rock face surface. Such a texture can lead to an overwhelming heaviness, but Richardson always relieved it by using several colors of stone to distract the eye.

Another prominent characteristic is his drive for horizontality in his designs. Whereas the norm was for buildings to reach upwards, he also attempted to place them in unison with the surface of the ground.

Perhaps the subtlest touch of all was the academic believability of his designs, as opposed to some of the fantastic piles of stone erected by others. One felt instinctively that his designs represented the way *real* Romanesque structures had been built.

Of all the houses built in Springfield and Clark County, none was ever actually done by Richardson, himself, although he built for Springfield clients. He did one house for Benjamin Warder in Washington, D.C., and another for J. J. Glessner (of Warder, Bushnell & Glessner) in Chicago. His successor firm, Shepley, Rutan & Coolidge, designed the Warder Public Library and then the Bushnell Building. It was one of his best imitators,

page 131

however, Robert H. Robertson, who designed the prestigious mansion of Asa S. Bushnell, Governor of Ohio 1888–1892. The Bushnell mansion is said to have cost $350,000 to build and gives a good idea of Richardsonian Romanesque design *(fig. 170, see next spread).*[9]

Once the concept of rock-faced masonry was popularized by Richardson, virtually every architect tried to design something in this fabric and sell it as "Romanesque." The usual result was to take an Eastlake or Queen Anne home and clothe it in stone, rather than brick or frame. In almost every case, the obligatory feature in the architect's view was the corner tower. Later the horseshoe arch became a required feature of the front entryway. One interesting, if not bizarre, innovation was the introduction of the "onion-shaped" dome/roof on the tower. It gives an almost Byzantine appearance to at least one corner of the house *(fig's. 171a, page 130, & 171b, at right, bottom).*

Perhaps the best, or at least most fascinating, of the Romanesque houses in Springfield is the last mansion built by industrialist P.P. Mast, on West High Street, in 1882–1883 *(see figure 171a, previous page).* The mass of the prodigious pile of stone is Eastlake in concept, but with much eclecticism, also. The square tower is Eastlake, but it has Renaissance window caps and Neoclassical swags at the third floor level. The standard Eastlake porch is here reproduced in stone, even to imitation cutouts and brackets. One gable is filled, in Eastlake

[9] *For much of its history the mansion was attributed to Richardson, based on a misinterpreted monogram carved on a pillar. This was not corrected until the later 1960s.*

174. *The Edward Wren House, 1115 North Limestone Street, 1889.*

style, the other done in quasi-Stick style. The arched, triplet windows are Queen Anne, as is the front tower, while the windows in it are Eastlake, the dome Byzantine and the open arcading Renaissance. The arcading in the tower, by the way, duplicates that seen in his second house across the street, at West High and Jackson Streets *(see figure 124, page 89)*.

Here, obviously, there is no unity of design such as Richardson would have produced. Yet, it is undeniably such a fascinating and absorbing structure that one could spend a vast amount of time picking out all of the details. And that is just what the architect intended: a picturesque house that would hold the viewer's attention. Of almost equal fascination is the Judge Hagan house, built about 1895–1896 at Center and Euclid Streets. This is the very paradigm of a Queen Anne house *(fig. 171b, right, below)*; in fact, it is almost a caricature of the style.

For those wanting more than a frame Queen Anne home, but not the ruinous expense and difficulties of a stone house, brick was the only alternative. Throughout the 1880s and 1890s, numbers of large brick homes were constructed in Springfield, almost uniformly of dark red "Philadelphia" brick with stone trim. Occasionally a little arcading, a la Richardson, was attempted, but on the whole they adhered closely to Queen Anne stylistics. Some of the more prominent of these are the Phelps House *(see figure 168a, page 128)* now razed, the Ross Mitchell House, 302 East High Street *(fig. 172, at top)*, and the two houses designed by Robert Gotwald at 505 and 515 North Fountain Avenue *(see figures 181a, page 147, & 181b, page 145)*.

An interesting variant on the style of these homes is the passion of the later 1880s for things German, or Flemish, which was manifested across the United States by the use of such gables on houses. Two well-known examples of this locally are the W. S. Thomas mansion on East High Street *(fig. 173, page 136)*, and the former Edward Wren Home on North Limestone Street *(fig. 174, at left)*.

fig. 172

171b (below). The Judge Hagan House, Center and Euclid Streets, built ca. 1896. Note the bulbous "onion" dome on the tower, a similarity it shared with the Mast House.
172 (above). The Ross Mitchell House, 302 East High Street, built ca. 1891–94. This old photograph was taken before a second story was added to the front porch and High Street was widened.
174 (at left). The Edward Wren House, 1115 North Limestone Street, as it appeared in Springfield Illustrated, 1889.

fig. 171b

170 The Asa Bushnell mansion, 838 East High Street, designed by Robert H. Robertson, the leading interpreter of H. H. Richardson's style, in 1888.

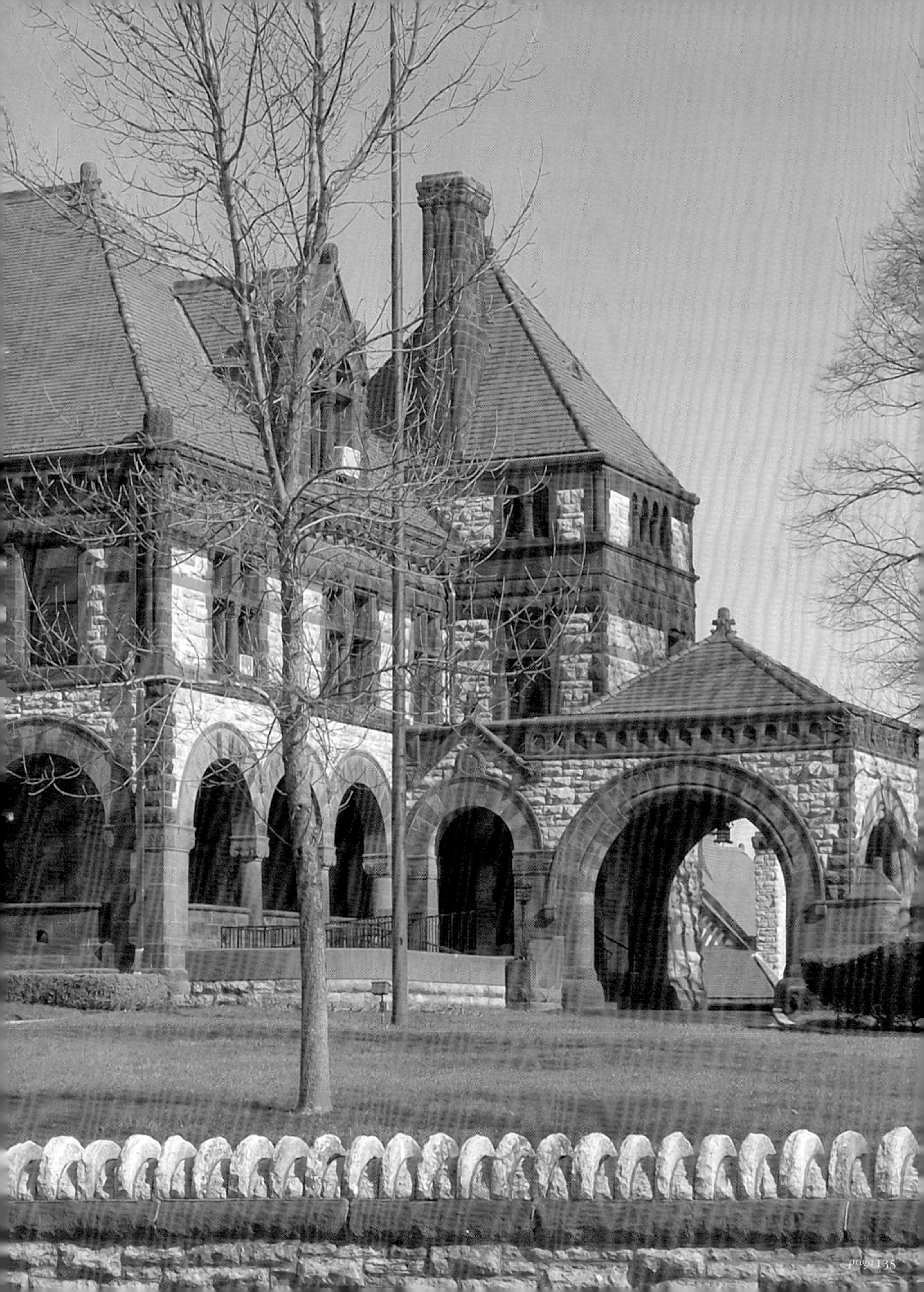

173 *The W. S. Thomas House, 721 East High St., from Springfield Illustrated, 1889.*

The last of the prominent styles of the period 1870–1893 has been called the "Shingle style," for lack of any better title. The name implies its reality—a house covered with shingles, although not every specimen is entirely so. As has often been said, European builders and architects rarely clothed their homes completely in shingles. But seventeenth-century New England settlements found that shingles withstood harsh winters far better than siding and paint. Thus, shingled exterior walls became common in those early seaboard areas.

In the very late 1870s, a few eastern architects began to resurrect this principle and apply it to both Queen Anne and Romanesque houses—for picturesque effect, of course. By the mid 1880s, a hybrid style had evolved through the interaction of the shingle on the two styles of architecture. What evolved were massive houses with little exterior decoration (fig. 175a, next page). The size of windows was reduced and they are often found in multiples in casements, while towers no longer boldly projected from corners. In fact, external smoothness and rotundity of surface became the hallmark of the new mode (fig. 175b, next page).

On the interior, the Victorian concept of compartmentalization of rooms and areas gave way to an openness and unification. Even Richardson designed in this fashion, although he did not like to do private homes and preferred to work in stone.

The style took some time to penetrate from the east even as far as Ohio. Most of those built in Springfield and Clark County were not erected until the mid- to late-1890s. Examples are not profuse, but lightly scattered over the city. In the period 1930–1940 a few "Colonial Revival" houses (fig. 176, above) were built in Springfield in a shingled style. These have little in common with those of the nineteenth century—except for the shingles!

173 (at left). The W. S. Thomas House, 721 East High St., as it appeared soon after construction, from Springfield Illustrated, 1889. 176 (above). Colonial Revival house sheathed in wooden shingles, 2349 E. High St. This design, popular ca. 1920–40, copies the eighteenth-century originals, not the 1880s Shingle style.

With the rise of first the Eastlake, and then the Queen Anne house, the American passion for emulating or imitating regal French or Italian architecture seemed to pass. The success of Henry Hobson Richardson and his French Romanesque appears at first glance to be a retrograde movement. Yet Richardson's designs were principally for public buildings. The few private homes he created were exclusively for people of great wealth and could be appreciated only by people who had little else to do in life, or who wished merely to be ostentatious with their money. Richardson's major domestic contribution was in his excellent shingle designs that could be adapted for the average homeowner.[10]

While earlier eras in American architecture had dwelt on creating homes that inspired aesthetic reflections, or visions of grandeur, the Eastlake and Queen Anne witnessed a shift to thoughts of warmth, comfort and solid pleasure. Such homes were commonly fitted not only with early versions of modern heating, light and sanitation, but also featured that pleasant device, the inglenook.

The inglenook was a small alcove, fitted with a fireplace, and sometimes benches or settles, where a visitor could warm himself upon first entering a house, and before proceeding to the main rooms. It was quaint, picturesque and—by modern standards—an expensive luxury. Yet it denoted a very human outlook in architecture. Americans had settled into ersatz-Mediaeval comfort, as the huge number of Queen Anne homes in Springfield testifies. What more could the public want?

[10]*See remarks on the Dimond House, p.116.*

175a (below). Carriage House, Bushnell Mansion, 838 East High Street, ca. 1888. The structure is in something of a modified Shingle style. 175b (background screen). The M. F. Stoughton House, Cambridge, Massachusetts, designed in the true Shingle style by H. H. Richardson in 1883.

fig. 175a

East High Street

The year 1848 was a most important one for Springfield's future growth. The original Market House, built on Main Street at Fisher, was replaced by a new brick structure at Market and High Streets. The first floor of the building had market stalls and the second floor was used for public meetings and as a city hall. The boundaries of Market Street were also moved back, so as to create a true Market Square. Springfield was coming of age and innumerable dignitaries would appear at the building over the next forty years. South Market Street would benefit immensely from this development.

At the same time, the brothers William and Gustavus Foos bought a block of ninety acres on the south side of East High Street, the Chillicothe Road, and made an addition to the city.

Their lots, numbered 604–646, ran eastward, from approximately where the Mad River & Lake Erie Railroad crossed High Street, to East Street, then called "Township Road." While this area would be slower to develop than South Market Street (Fountain Avenue), it would become the most favored and prestigious area within the city.

Neither South Fountain Avenue in the 1870s, nor West High Street in the 1880s would be able to dislodge it from its position as the premier neighborhood in Springfield.

Somewhat like the several streets above and paralleling Buck Creek, and running from Limestone eastward, this street had already begun to be thought of in terms of suburban growth, along the lines advocated by A. J. Downing. By 1852, pioneer druggist John Ludlow had built a suburban estate on East High Street, just one block beyond the city limits. Ludlow was also involved with the Springfield Bank and would soon become its president. The W. H. Beers and Company *History of Clark County* stated that, "the home of Mr. Ludlow is just outside the city limits in an elegant residence of the Elizabethan style of architecture, his grounds being equal to any in the city." Then and now, such an estate was most appropriate to a successful banker-businessman.

William Rockel's *20th Century History of Springfield and Clark County* reports, in regard to Gustavus Foos, that, "In this year (1848) the brothers bought a large tract of land at Springfield which they laid out in town lots and these now form the best residence sections in the city." In the section on William Foos, however, there is a different tone. No doubt, this is a reflection of the subject, the very successful banker and Leffel Company officer. The entry relates that, "In association with his brother, the late Gustavus Foos, he bought a large tract of land for a merely nominal sum, and this is now one of the most valuable additions of Springfield. It was but one of his many successful enterprises."

Gustavus Foos and brother William Foos (of whom no photo is known to exist), were the original developers of East High St.

SECTION & WARD MAP OF Springfield 1894

The same book, then, tells the story two ways. Gustavus thought of East High Street in terms of buyer satisfaction. He was the dreamer, who could not stand being locked up in a bank job for eight hours a day. William was the smart one, a hard-headed businessman. He thought of East High Street in terms of seller satisfaction. Springfield was fortunate to have both men available to stimulate its growth in two ways at the same time—like the Roman god Janus.

Due to its extended period of growth, roughly 1850 to 1900, East High Street was the home to a variety of men and women who built houses on it. Its lifespan breaks down into several phases illustrated by the builders and their architecture.

The western portion, which belongs more to the downtown of Springfield, would see the relatively primitive home of Jeremiah Warder, early land entrepreneur at 406 East High Street. Ross Mitchell, however, would intrude at a late date, demolish a house and build a grandiose mansion (*see figure 172, page 133*).

The central section would be the area for high Victorian architectural and society growth. All of the prominent manufacturers would build mansions here, including John Foos, Asa Bushnell, William Thomas, and E. C. Middleton (later occupied by William Warder). (*See figures 108, page 81; 170, page 135; 173, page 136; & 136a & b, pages 98-99, respectively.*)

With the exception of the Pringle-Patric and Phillips mansions at 1316 & 1320 East High Street, the eastern portion of the street would see the downsizing of houses into just large homes. John Bushnell, John Hoppess, and many others would create comfortable retreats, more than social statements.

Flexible people are the ones who survive. Perhaps this is true for streets, also.

East High Street was once the most prestigious address in Springfield and the home to the city's captains of industry and their families. An 1894 map shows the expansion in all directions of the residential areas of Springfield.

Eclectual

TURN BACKWARD,

When a visitor strolled the avenues of the Centennial Exposition at Philadelphia in the summer of 1876, he or she was regaled with a fairyland vision. On all sides was presented a profusion of different building types *(fig. 177, at right)*, from vast structures in the monumental styles fashionable in Paris and Berlin, to the modest huts of exotic islanders. Individual states of the Union had their own buildings, which were created in all the varying eclectic forms of the later nineteenth century, including Ohio's in the newly popular Eastlake mode.

But what may have attracted the visitor's attention most was a modest building known as the "New England Farmhouse." Here an attempt had been made to recreate a typical, pre-Revolution farmhouse and furnish it with relics going as far back as *Mayflower* days *(fig. 178, immediate left))*. Not only was the exhibit immensely popular as a curiosity, it also provoked some to thought. Although the Exhibition grounds offered virtually every known style of architecture, the "New England Farmhouse" was the only item that was even vaguely "American" in design. For a few it mattered greatly that a nation emerging into worldwide importance, such as the United States, should have its *own* national architecture.

The seed had been planted, but it took some time for it to germinate. The balance of the 1870s would see the rise of the Eastlake and then its metamorphosis into the Queen Anne of the 1880s *(fig's. 179a, below, & 179b, at left)*. At the same time, H. H. Richardson and others would be raising immense piles of stone into that most un-American of all

177 (above). The State Headquarters, Centennial Exposition, Philadelphia, from Harper's Weekly, June 3, 1876. 178 (immediate left). New England farmhouse kitchen at the Centennial Exposition, Harper's, June 3, 1876. 179a (screen, below). Design for a small inn, from Horticulturist magazine, edited by A. J. Downing, 1846–52. 179b (far left). The Winchell House, 635 East High Street, built ca. 1892. Compare to the Downing design (below) of forty years earlier.

TURN BACKWARD

chapter THIRTEEN

182 The Robert Rogers House, 1563 East High Street, ca. 1900.

styles, Romanesque. But, by the late 1880s, a few architects had begun to publish details of Colonial houses in which they had taken an interest.

H. H. Richardson had died in 1886 and the Romanesque began its decline at about the same time, although a few men, such as Robert H. Robertson and Charles Cregar of Springfield, continued to turn out creditable work in that idiom. For most, however, it was becoming an uninspired dead-end. Both a new style and an impetus were becoming necessary to revitalize the architecture scene.

The impetus came first. The year 1892 would be the four-hundredth anniversary of the discovery of America by Columbus. The idea of a "Columbian Exposition" to mark the anniversary took the public's fancy and, after much competition, Chicago won the honor of hosting the celebration. Under the leadership of architect Daniel Burnham, a board was assembled of some of the most important architects in the country, including the prestigious firm of McKim, Mead & White of New York. These latter had already, as early as 1877, made an extensive file and reference collection of drawings of selected New England homes.

What emerged from their planning was a new fairyland. Unlike Philadelphia in 1876, the major architecture was no longer that of European capitals. Instead, hundreds of acres were filled with majestic structures created in a resuscitated Graeco-Roman style. It was as though Ancient Rome and Georgian America had been combined for the embellishment of huge exhibition buildings. The Second Neoclassical period had been born ☼ (fig. 180, right).

Following the Exposition, what had been merely a fad of the rich became a serious movement: reproduction of colonial architecture. Architects such as Charles McKim and Stanford White, like Richardson, had attended the *Ecole des Beaux-Arts*. Thus their Colonial Revival designs had a highly archaeological approach. Some of their creations can scarcely be differentiated from the original eighteenth-century models.

Yet McKim, Mead & White was not the only firm with men who had studied in Paris. By the time of the Columbian Exposition in 1893, numerous architects had studied abroad, or in America under European instructors. Richard Morris Hunt, ten years older than Richardson, had preceded him to the *Ecole* and arrived home first. By 1890, Hunt was designing the most extravagant mansions in America, for the wealthiest of the wealthy—especially the Vanderbilts. His particular forte, the direct product of his European sojourn, was fantastic villas in a sixteenth-century French Chateau style—but he was equally proficient at Genoese palazzos!

These men and others had preceded the Exposition in their early efforts, but it was the Columbian Exposition in all its concentrated massiveness that brought home to Americans the concept of *archaeologically correct* revivalism, as opposed to the romanticized efforts

fig. 180

180 (above). *The Ohio Building, Columbian Exposition. A good example of the newly popular Georgian Revival style.* 182 (far left). *The Robert Rogers House, 1563 East High Street, built ca. 1900. Note the use of Queen Anne stylistics, as well as Colonial Revival design.* 181b (below). *Dr. D. K. Gotwald House, 505 North Fountain Avenue, designed by Robert Gotwald, 1894.*

181b *Dr. D. K. Gotwald House, 505 North Fountain Avenue, 1894.*

183a *J. S. Crowell mansion, 1127 East High Street, built ca. 1904–05.*

of the earlier nineteenth century. From 1893 onward it became perfectly acceptable to design a simple home, or a vast mansion in any historical style, provided it was done correctly.

For approximately the next fifteen to twenty years, architects designed homes in almost every conceivable historical mode, from German castles to Georgian mansions. Due to this huge variety it is extremely difficult to find a name for the era. Some of the proposed titles are: Neoclassical Revival, Second Neoclassical, Neoclassical, Georgian Revival, Colonial Revival, and *Beaux Arts*, not to mention Second Renaissance Revival. Each of these names has a certain validity, since it describes types of buildings designed during the period; yet it were better if there were one name for the whole, and the best candidate is *Beaux Arts*. All of the various sub-styles created during the era are directly or indirectly the product of a training instituted by that famous school.

While castles, chateaux and palazzos serve well as national monuments or great landmarks, they are affordable to only a minute fraction of the population. They also suffer from the disability of not being capable of reduction to a size within the purse of an ordinary family–or even one of moderate means.

On the other hand, Georgian/Neoclassical/Colonial designs had originated in houses of innumerable different sizes and shapes. There was something for every pocketbook. In addition, their use of Graeco-Roman decoration preserved them from being *dated* to one particular era. In short, they were *flexible*, and that is the secret of *classicism*. Thus, while wealth might attempt to imitate the palaces of real or fancied European ancestors, the average American was resurrecting a real or adopted colonial past for his new home. Colonial Revival became the national design and has remained so to the present day, despite the various manias for "Ranch Homes," "A-Frames," "Geodesic Domes," etc., etc.

By the decade of the 1890s, most Springfielders of means had erected their family mansions. Those who did build continued to use the now standard Queen Anne manner. If the house was of some pretension, it was usually built, as mentioned above, of smooth red brick with stone embellishments. By 1891 Robert Gotwald had become one of the prominent architects in Springfield and was responsible for many of these larger brick homes (fig's. 181a, at right, & 181b, page 145), as well as a number of commercial structures, including the two Zimmerman Buildings and the old Gotwald/M & M Building.

About 1900, one Robert Rogers erected a house at 1563 East High Street (fig. 182, page 144), which offers a fascinating glimpse of the transition process in architecture. The first floor, built both of rock-faced stone and frame, features a curving bay and a stone porch in a generalized Romanesque-Queen Anne form. The second floor is basically Queen Anne, but the dormers and detailing are Colonial Revival. Very appropriately, this is sometimes called the "Shirtwaist style,"

fig. 185

181a (immediately below). Former home of Prof. Robert Remsberg, 515 North Fountain Avenue, designed by Robert Gotwald, 1892.
183a (at left). J. S. Crowell mansion, 1127 East High Street, built ca. 1904–05.
183b (at bottom). Iris Gardens behind the Crowell mansion when it was acquired by Paul C. Martin, from Artwork of Springfield, Ohio, 1927.
185 (above). The Tittle Apartments, corner of North Limestone and Cassilly Streets, ca. 1913–14.

fig. 181a

183b *Iris Gardens behind the Crowell mansion when it was acquired by Paul C. Martin.*

page 147

No Place Like Home | Turn Backward, Turn Backward

184 *The Gus Sun House, 840 North Fountain Avenue, ca. 1910–11.*

page 149

188 *Colonial Revival home of J. A. Linn, 16 East Home Road, ca. 1911.*

after the women's fashion of wearing a plain tailored blouse above a skirt of a radically contrasting material, such as wool.

At about the same time, J. S. Crowell, of publishing fame, broke fashion by building a completely Georgian Revival mansion at 1127 East High Street ❀ *(fig. 183a, page 146)*. In every respect the house is a perfect example of the style. It was later acquired by attorney Paul C. Martin, who added flower gardens, especially iris, until the grounds were the most beautifully landscaped in Springfield, or the county ❀ *(fig. 183b, page 147)*. The gardens have long since been removed and the building now houses the Greek Orthodox Church.

Somewhat later, in 1910 or 1911, entertainment entrepreneur Gus Sun built a large home at the southeast corner of Fountain and Cassilly Streets. This is a rather interesting specimen, since he combined the general lines of the then already old-fashioned "Bridged Chimney Late Federal" style with Georgian detailing, including a grand portico ✦ *(fig. 184, previous spread)*. It is now the home of Sigma Kappa sorority.

About two years later, in 1913 or 1914, another Classical Revival was built only a block away, at Limestone and Cassilly: the Tittle Apartments ✦ *(fig. 185, page 147)*. The lofty columns of the Tittle Apartments clearly mark it as Classical/Georgian in style. Yet there is a second element present in the design that was becoming increasingly popular in the first two decades of the twentieth century—Japanese influence.

After the first mass exposure to things Japanese at the Centennial Exposition in 1876, persons of refinement and education swiftly came to love the arts of the East. A curious dichotomy arose whereby a person might live in a revival home of quasi-Old World design, and yet load the interior with Oriental art and decorations. The contrast between the two worlds was devastating, yet this only added to the "picturesqueness" of the effect. Part of the Japanese Movement included the adoption of extremely deep eaves with a slight curve in the pitch of the roof, and the whole covered with red tiles, like a Japanese temple. Some architects had in mind more the deep eaves of the Swiss chalet house type, but the result was basically the same.

One of the last of the large, pillared Colonial style homes to be built in Springfield was the House & Myers home at 1076 East High Street. Constructed about 1918 for the widows of Drs. House and Myers, the structure was an enlarged version of the simple Colonial box with a large portico attached ✦ *(fig. 186, at right, bottom)*. The massive first-floor Palladian windows were a somewhat unusual touch. The house has been demolished in more recent years.

For the average family, an extensive portico was an unnecessary luxury. Their homes were but simplified forms of Crowell mansions and amounted to lightly decorated boxes. Figure 187 *(above)* represents what, typically, was being built in Springfield up to about 1920. The house is frame and of two stories. The windows are very simple rectangles, although in this particular case the second floor has an interesting variant on the triple form Palladian window that was customary. A small, quasi-Colonial portico does not afford much protection from the weather, but it does give a "Colonial" effect. The roof has wide eaves that

fig. 187

186 (below). The House & Myers residence, 1076 East High Street, built 1918, now razed. 187 (above). Typical Colonial Revival house built for an average family, up to about 1920; 1007 North Limestone Street. 188 (at left). Colonial Revival home of J. A. Linn, 16 East Home Road, ca. 1911.

fig. 186

page 151

rest on very flat brackets, which, like the Chippendale pediment on the attic dormer, contribute to the overall effect. The best touch of all is the wooden, board pilasters at the corners.

This house exists in a multitude of variations, infinite in number, throughout Springfield, as well as the whole country. While not exhibiting the exact archaeological correctness of expensive mansions, still they are close enough to offer a taste of the Colonial combined with the comfort and spaciousness of the larger Victorian home.

Perhaps the greatest problem houses of this type have faced is painting. The Columbian Exposition was dubbed the "White City," because all of the major buildings were painted a brilliant, dazzling white. Contrary to what is often printed, the Exposition buildings were not constructed of stone. Their exterior walls were uniformly prepared by spreading cement-like stucco, called *staff*, over wooden lathing. At best, these were magnificent, but temporary exhibition buildings only. The only survivor, The Fine Arts Palace, *was* reconstructed in stone in the 1920s through a generous bill bequest. Today it houses The Museum of Science and Industry.

This overwhelming use of white, originally intended to imitate stone, seems to have convinced the public that there was no color to paint a house other than white. Up to that time, Victorian homes had usually been painted in several shades of earthy colors. The all-white exterior of Classical/Georgian Revival homes, but also all others, hides architectural details, blends one house with another and gives neighborhoods a boring uniformity. And modern research has shown that Colonial homes were originally painted in any of several pastel colors, in addition to white. The use of a two-color system as on the house in Figure 186 (previous page) highlights the true character of the home.

189 *The Colonial Revival home of Mrs. Gustavus Raup, 1845 North Fountain Boulevard, 1917–18.*

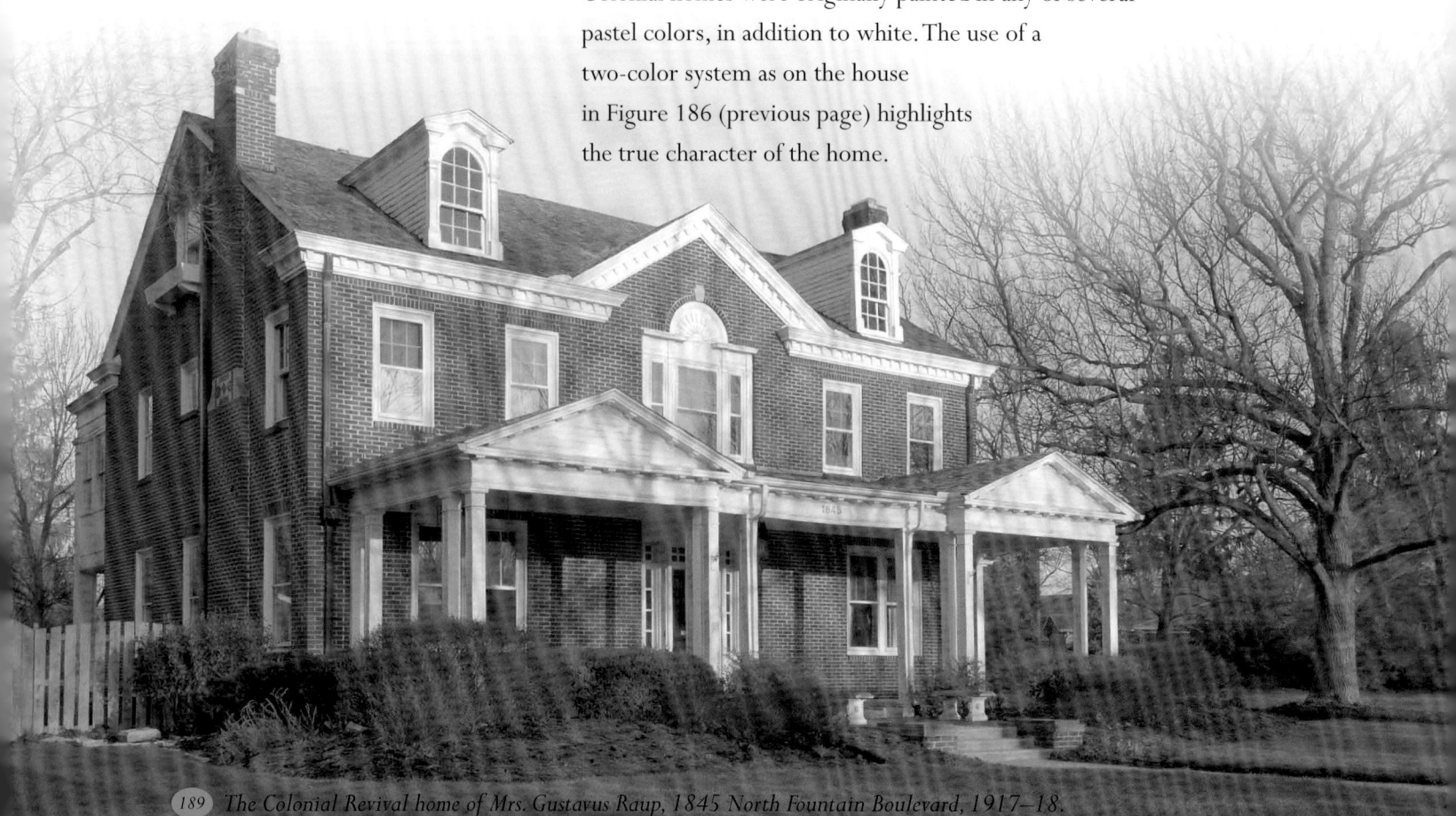

Boxes, of course, do not suit every taste and they are liable to excessive formality. In 1911, James A. Linn, vice-president of the Springfield Publishing Co., built a new home at the extreme northern edge of the city, where Fountain Boulevard intersects Home Road—then, Children's Home Road (fig. 188, page 150). He chose neither a box, nor a mansion like that of Crowell or Sun. Instead, he built a large, comfortable vernacular form of Colonial Revival. With its vergeboards in the dormers, bracketed side porches and struts in the main eaves, the house was almost a reversion to later nineteenth-century types.

At about the same time that Linn was building his home, a new architect entered the Springfield scene—Marley Lethly. Lethly's forte seems to have been Federal styling. In 1917–1918 he designed the new home of Mrs. Gustavus Raup, at 1845 North Fountain Boulevard (fig. 189, at left). The detail work on the dormers, eaves and central Palladian window display a high degree of talent. But it is his double porch, which is quite unusual. Apparently he was trying to refrain from blocking the view of—and from—his lovely window at center. A porch with pediment was desired, so his passion for symmetry allowed no choice but to double the pediment and thereby balance the dormers, a solution as difficult as the problem!

A house of equally fine Federal styling is the Luther Buchwalter house, built about 1916–1917 at 2132 East High Street (fig. 190, above, right). Not only is all of the detailing crisp and precise, but the house features "blind arcading" in the first floor with *lunettes* over the windows. This is a feature much used by Charles Bulfinch in Boston homes, over a century earlier.

These and many dozens more throughout the neighborhoods of Springfield represent America's first true attempt to discover an architectural form that was indigenous to the country and symbolic of the nation and its aspirations. Yet the fact could not be hidden that it was not truly a native style, that it had been borrowed essentially from England. For some people this was, no doubt, merely academic hair-splitting. The style represented America at its most eloquent and the period of this revival, 1892 to about 1918, was an era of growing prestige on the world scene for the United States.

The rest between the Spanish-American War and World War I provided an ideal ground for the seeds of remembrance. Yet there were undercurrents in this placid-appearing pool. Some were searching for things more "picturesque" than stuffy old Colonial homes; others were still striving to find or invent a national architecture. Among these latter, the most famous, Frank Lloyd Wright, would build a radically unconventional home for an unconventional Springfielder, Burton J. Westcott.

fig. 190

189 (at left). The Colonial Revival home of Mrs. Gustavus Raup, 1845 North Fountain Boulevard, designed by Marley Lethly, 1917–18.
190 (above). The Luther Buchwalter House, 2132 East High Street, built ca. 1916–17.

Robert C. Gotwald

The first of the Gotwald family to arrive in Springfield was Dr. Luther A. Gotwald, who had been born in York County, Pennsylvania in 1833. At the age of ten his father died and he became an active supporter of his mother and seven siblings, becoming a clerk and later a printer. By 1852 he had managed to attend the preparatory school for the ministry, at Wittenberg College. Three years later he graduated from Pennsylvania College at Gettysburg in 1857, and the Lutheran Seminary there in 1859.

Upon receiving his license to preach, Gotwald served as pastor in a number of churches in Pennsylvania and Ohio. In 1885 he accepted a call to a church in Springfield and here he spent the balance of his life. He is credited with founding Third, Fourth, Fifth, and Calvary Lutheran Churches. Dr. Gotwald likewise held a number of offices in the Lutheran Church and taught at Wittenberg College.

Luther Gotwald married Mary E. King, sister of a successful Springfield merchant, David King, in 1859. That marriage produced nine children, several of whom died young. Probably the best known of those who reached adulthood were Dr. D. King, M.D. and Robert C., an architect.

Robert C. Gotwald was born in 1864, when his father held a church at Lebanon, Pennsylvania. As a youth he attended the York County Academy and Pennsylvania College. He graduated from Lehigh University with a degree in Civil Engineering, in 1886, at the age of twenty-two. He immediately went west and took a job in the bridge-building department of the Missouri Pacific Railroad for five years. At the end of that time, in 1891, he returned to Springfield and opened an architectural office. Apparently his railroad, bridge-building experience convinced him that if he could design something to support a locomotive and cars, he could certainly design a house.

Gotwald's return to Springfield was well-timed. Local architectural genius Charles Cregar was at the pinnacle of his career, but would die very soon, as a young man. That would only increase the architectural vacuum in Springfield. People of means, who could afford an architect, had already begun turning to outside help. It was a good time for a talented newcomer to arrive.

Most of Gotwald's identified surviving early work is in a fairly standard Queen Anne style. If he was the architect for Ross Mitchell's new home on East High Street, the German dormer on the otherwise routine corner tower was a stroke of genius. However, some brickwork on the house suggests Cregar's touch (*see figure 172, page 133*).

On the other hand, the three homes Gotwald built for relatives at 505 and 515 North Fountain Avenue (*see figures 181a, page 147, & b, page145*), and around the corner (which burned in 2006) are like the railroad bridges with which he was so familiar. They are big, strong and plain, built out of conventional material (dark red Philadelphia brick) in a fairly conventional design.

Gotwald would go on to have a large number of commercial and residential clients. Over the years his career somewhat paralleled Cregar's, including several churches, and a synagogue. Despite prolific careers, no photo is known of either of Springfield's most prominent nineteenth-century architects. Also like Cregar, he had the opportunity to design a public building, the West County, or today, the A. B. Graham Building.

On the exterior, the A. B. Graham is a *tour de force* of *Beaux Arts*

Classicism. Erected in 1901, the building is in the form of a Roman triumphal arch with office wings on either side. Much of the exterior decorative work was done in the then-popular baked terra cotta.

The interior of the building was finished in the cold, stark style so prevalent at the time, with marble slab wainscoting and oak woodwork. The great focal point of the structure is the grand staircase going from the first to second floor (*see figure 205a, page 165*). The actual marble steps are framed by a cast-iron balustrade.

Although technically in an Art Nouveau style, this ironwork is highly reminiscent of that advocated by Louis Sullivan, especially in his work on the (now) Carson Pirie Scott Building in downtown Chicago (*see figure 205b, page 164*).

Gotwald's career would continue for many years and he would be involved in a wide array of projects. These cover the full range of an architect's work, from the Boathouse in Snyder Park to elegant residences in Ridgewood (*see figure 188, page 150*). Interestingly, though, like Cregar, it is his early work on the A. B. Graham Building and the North Fountain Avenue houses that is remembered today as quintessential Robert Gotwald.

Background screen, at left—The New Zimmerman Building once stood on the northwest corner of Main and Limestone Sts., now a parking lot. Bottom left—The former West County Building, now known as the A. B. Graham Building, located on the southwest corner of Columbia and Limestone Sts. Above—The Carnegie Science Hall, now known simply as Carnegie Hall, on the Wittenberg University campus. Below, and left—The Gotwald Building, later known as the M&M Bank Building, which was located on the southeast corner of Main and Limestone Sts.

Sullivan
PARES CUM PARIBUS

The title of this chapter, an elegant Latin phrase, which rolls from the tongue with a classical rhythm, hardly seems to fit the subject matter of Frank Lloyd Wright's architecture and its relation to Springfield, Ohio. Yet, as any elementary Latin student can tell you, very freely translated, it means, "Birds of a feather flock together." No phrase would seem to better describe the apparently diverse characters of Wright, his Springfield clients and the area itself. But like so many subjects, we cannot start at what appears to be the beginning; we must go backward a few steps.

LOUIS HENRI SULLIVAN was born in Boston in 1856. At the appropriate age he entered the Massachusetts Institute of Technology, where he began to study architecture. He did not complete his work there; instead, like Richardson and others, he decamped for Paris and the *Ecole des Beaux-Arts,* where he studied and then served as apprentice to a Parisian architect.

Returning to the United States, he became a draftsman for the respected Chicago architect Dankmar Adler in 1879. After a brilliant display of talent he became Adler's partner in 1881. Six years later, the firm was able to secure the commission for the grandiose Auditorium Theatre and Hotel ✹ *(fig. 191, at right),* one of the most important architectural undertakings of the era.

Only one year before, in 1886, Richardson had started the Marshall Field Wholesale Building in Chicago—and then died. After Sullivan had inspected Richardson's designs, and then published them, he completely revised his own initial drawings for the Auditorium Building. Instead of a massive but fairly conventional Romanesque-Queen Anne style of structure of rock-faced masonry, replete with innumerable towers and turrets, the building was stripped of most exterior decoration.

191 (above). The Auditorium Building, Chicago, designed by Louis Sullivan, constructed 1887–89. Note the amount of window space and decreasing exterior decoration. 205b (left). Louis Sullivan iron scrollwork, Schlessinger & Meyer department store, now Carson Pirie Scott & Co., Chicago. Inset at right is detail from the painting, "Meeting of the Board of Architects and the Grounds and Buildings Committee."

CONGREGANTUR

hapter FOURTEEN

192 (above). The Schiller Theater building. Chicago; designed by Louis Sullivan. The cupola area on the top of the structure resembles that on his Transportation Building.
194 (below). "The Breakers," Newport, R.I., designed by Richard M. Hunt, is typical of the revival mansions built for the wealthy in the Gilded Age. In this case, the palazzo was built for Cornelius Vanderbilt.

Even more interesting was his emphasis on the technical aspects of the structure, especially his increasing tendency to carry the weight of the building downwards on iron and stone columns and piers. He was abandoning the ancient, venerated and traditional method of letting the exterior walls carry the load and transferred to them through cross members. The result, of course, was to allow for increased height in a structure without increasing the thickness of the walls to ridiculous proportions. But perhaps the greatest lesson Sullivan learned from Richardson's project was the newly rediscovered concept of letting as much light as possible into a building by enlarging the window space and reducing the exterior walls to a minimal support and dividing function.[11]

During the next four years, from 1887–1891, Sullivan continued to refine the ideas he had expressed in the Auditorium Building. As he later admitted, he was much under the domination of the mid nineteenth-century sculptor and essayist, Horatio Greenough. Although the latter had worked and written during the Greek Revival period, and was a tremendous success with his sculpture, *The Greek Slave*, he was much more interested in the abstract principles of Greek art and architecture. Sullivan reformulated Greenough's ideas into the famous and often-recalled phrase, "Form follows function."

Keeping Greenough's dicta in mind, Sullivan developed his architectural style in two very different directions. His buildings tended to have increasingly "clean" lines, devoid of all projecting decoration. They also began to utilize the concept of an iron/steel framework with the exterior walls as merely an enclosing curtain. This allowed them to rise to unprecedented heights *(fig. 192, left)*.

At the same time that these very modern trends arose, Sullivan also came under the influence of the popular *Art Nouveau* style of decoration. This new form of artwork made great use of natural motifs, e.g., plants, flowers and insects. It was not, however, a realistic portrayal of nature, but rather an exaggerated or distorted vision. Leaves and stems often blended together, or else strained to unnatural height. In some cases plants underwent stylization and became abstracted. Even today one can see this most easily in churches built between 1890 and 1910. In some largely ignored nook there is a small window with a pale-colored flower, hardly distinguishable from the stained-glass sections comprising the whole window.

Sullivan took this style and reworked it in his own mold, creating an entirely unique style of decoration. The resulting product was in the form

---
[11] *The same principle had evolved during the period in which the Gothic cathedral had been perfected, the twelfth–sixteenth centuries.*

of a crowded band of low relief sculpture or metalwork. Plant forms became highly abstracted into Rococo swirls that intertwined and strained against each other. By tight grouping and repetition, such bands, when viewed at a distance, gave almost the effect of a simple geometric panel, which still had great richness about it.

In the winter of 1890–1891, plans got underway for the Columbian Exposition in Chicago. Architects were contacted and eagerly accepted commissions for the various buildings. Sullivan and Adler obtained that for the Transportation Building. On February 24, 1891, there was a meeting of architects to view and discuss their various plans ❁ *(fig. 193, below)*. This Board of Architects was heavily weighted with the prestigious eastern forms which had been building Classical Revival mansions for the wealthy ❁ *(fig. 194, far left, bottom)*. The chairman was Daniel Burnham of Chicago, who apologized to the easterners for the crudeness of local architecture in comparison with their refined products. By the end of the day, Sullivan was horrified; everything was to be done in Classical Revival. He considered it a near mortal blow to progressive architecture.[12] Yet Sullivan prevailed to a certain extent, and the Transportation Building was done in *his* style. Most guidebooks to the Exposition noted its rich and novel design, praising it greatly but stressing the unusual nature of the design, especially the fantastic portal, or "Golden Door," as it was called ❁ *(fig. 195, right, at top)*. A muted form of this doorway, with some Richardsonian influence, was used by Sullivan in his famous Peoples Federal Savings and Loan Association in Sidney, Ohio ❁ *(fig. 196, right, bottom)*.

The same feeling of unhappiness with the Exposition was felt by one of Sullivan's assistants, Frank Lloyd Wright, who had joined the firm in 1887, the same year that the design competition for the Auditorium Building was won by Sullivan. In 1893, after the Exposition had closed, Wright left Sullivan & Adler. Daniel Burnham wanted him to join his own firm, but Wright went his own way.

[12] Sullivan actually did not make public his reservations about the Columbian Exposition architecture until some thirty-six years later!

193 (near left). Painting, "Meeting of the Board of Architects and the Grounds and Buildings Committee," February 24, 1891; Sullivan is with dark beard, seated at table.
195 (above). The Transportation Building and its famous "Golden Door," by Louis Sullivan, Columbian Exposition, Chicago, 1893. Receding arches within a central arch was also a device used on mediaeval churches.
196 (below). The Peoples Federal Savings and Loan Association by Louis Sullivan, 101 E. Court St., Sidney, Ohio.

page 159

Although Wright revered Sullivan's message of "Form follows function," he had no feeling for Sullivan's brand of decoration—or for anyone else's, for that matter. Early in life Wright had become entranced with things Japanese, especially their architecture and scrolls. Developing a theory of a natural or organic house out of the simple rectilinear architecture of Japan *(fig. 197, right)*, Wright soon had his own style of home design.

Frank Lloyd Wright and his architecture are still being examined and probed today by the greatest experts. Their findings are beyond the scope of this work. Yet we can note that the theme of his early houses was open, uncluttered space. Wright's houses demanded the abolition of the traditional concept of rooms completely separated by doors. At the same time, Wright and others continued the handcrafts movement that had begun in England decades before, in the time of Eastlake. Interior furnishings were part of the total scheme of the design—like Robert Adam's idea—and much had to be built by hand by the most skilled carpenters on the site of each individual house. In like fashion, wood and brick were treated as objects of veneration and were never disguised as anything else. The whole structure was an "organic" or living thing, like nature, and each part had its own proper place and distinction.

Radically unconventional ideas such as Wright's could never win a quick clientele in Queen Anne America, much less the highly formalistic society of the 1890s. Clients had to be not only wealthy, but just as unconventional as Wright himself. Even as late as 1901, when several of his designs were published in *Ladies' Home Journal*, his practice does not seem to have been too large. Although the *Journal* had been publishing the most *avant-garde* home designs since 1895, the publicity did not bring him any additional clients. Wright's designs that were published in 1901 were prototypes for

no place like home | pares cum paribus congregantur

what he would soon denominate: "Prairie Houses," with their low, horizontal and rectilinear profile, which he felt were in harmony with the prairie lands of his Midwestern home in Illinois. Wright's coming to Springfield to build a "Prairie House" in a state of forests was no more unorthodox than anything else he ever did.

Burton J. Westcott (fig. 198, below, far left) was born at Richmond, Indiana, in 1868, the son of John Westcott, who manufactured farm implements in his Hoosier Drill Co. In 1903 Hoosier Drill merged with several other implement manufacturers to form the American Seeding Machine Co. (fig. 199, below, far left), and moved its executive offices to Springfield. Burton Westcott was the newly elected treasurer of the company and he and his wife Orpha also moved to Springfield. It appears that as early as the year after their arrival, Frank Lloyd Wright had been commissioned to design a home for them. In the first major publication of Wright's designs, in Germany in 1911, an unexecuted design for a home for the Westcotts is placed with other of his 1904 designs.

How the Westcotts became involved with Wright has never been satisfactorily explained. In a 1977 article for *Ohio History*, Prof. Stephen Siek speculated that Mrs. Westcott may have been familiar with Wright through the *Ladies' Home Journal*, or she may have visited Oak Park, Illinois, where Wright's studio was located and some of his earliest work was built. Such a visit might have occurred in conjunction with her husband's business activities. Mrs. Westcott, of whom no photograph is known at present, appears to have been a dynamic, progressive and somewhat liberated woman for her day, just the right sort of client for Wright!

No matter how the connection was made, it did not prove fruitful for several years. It was not until the summer of 1907 that Burton Westcott bought a lot from J. S. Crowell, at the northwest corner of

fig. 200

197 (at left, top). *Japanese Government Buildings, Columbian Exposition, Chicago, 1893. The presence of these structures probably helped to reinforce Wright's early concepts.*
198 (far left, bottom). *Burton J. Westcott, at the height of his career, ca. 1916.*
199 (left, bottom). *American Seeding Machine Company complex, Monroe, Gallagher and Mulberry Streets; drawing ca. 1916.*
200 (above). *The Westcott House, 1340 East High St. Probably in the summer of 1908.*
206 (below). *View of the Westcott Motor Car Co. complex. This drawing from about 1917 shows the company housed in the former P. P. Mast Co. factory at Warder and Spring Streets. The buildings would later house the Buckeye Incubator Co. It was razed for the Spring Street overpass.*

206 *Westcott Motor Car Co. complex, ca. 1917.*

page 161

207 *The Westcott House, ca. 1935-45.*

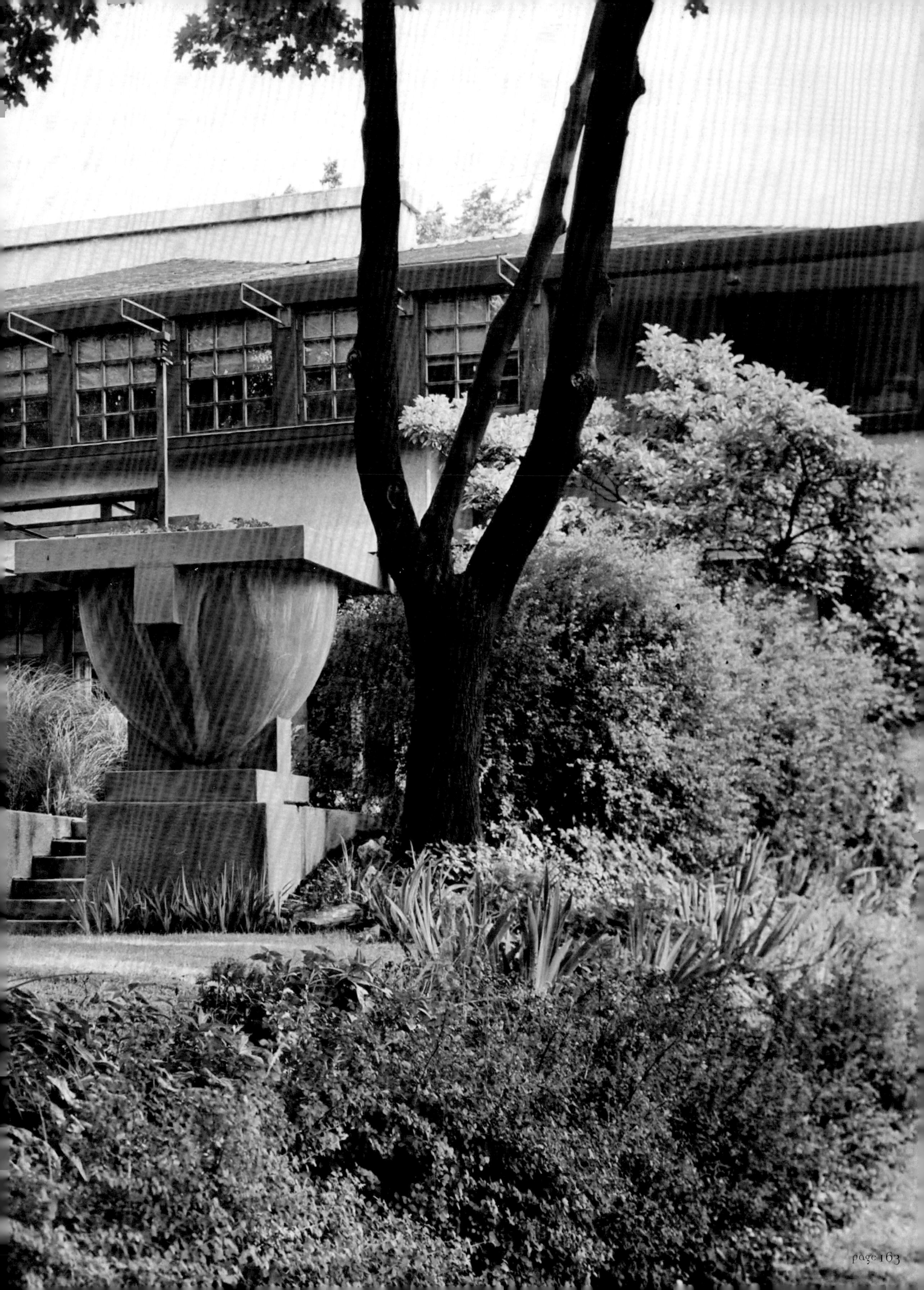

201 (at top). View of the three principal rooms across the front of the Westcott House, ca. 1908; the dining room is at the far end. 202 (above). Exterior view of the Westcott House in 1927, the year after Burton Westcott died. The house had been sold to Roscoe Pierce. The now-matured landscaping accents the Japanese appearance. From Artwork of Springfield, 1927. 205a (at far right). Grand staircase, A. B. Graham County Building, Limestone and Columbia Streets, Robert Gotwald, architect, 1901. 205b (background screen). Louis Sullivan iron scrollwork, Schlessinger & Meyer department store, now Carson Pirie Scott & Co., Chicago.

East High Street and Greenmount Avenue for his new home. Construction began in October 1907, but by then the house had been completely redesigned by Wright. Again, the reason is not known, but may be nothing more than the maturing of his abilities in the three-year-plus hiatus.

Construction continued on the house into 1908, at least (fig. 200, page 161). The 1909 City Directory lists the Westcotts at that address, but the directory would have been drawn up in advance, and the entry may have been wishful thinking. Twice that summer there were minor fires in the house, which, in the newspaper accounts, was "being erected" by Westcott. Therefore, the family probably did not move in until the later fall of 1908, at the earliest.

Wright published a view of what the completed exterior of the house would look like in the *Architectural Record* in 1908. The landscaping, however, does not conform to his designs published in 1911. Yet, those 1911 designs were apparently unrevised 1904 plans. Suffice it to say, the landscaping designs may have been revised several times. In fact, the Westcott House is considered to have received the most extensive landscaping treatment of any of Wright's "Prairie Houses."

A gauge of Orpha Westcott's interest may be that it was not until the fall of 1911, when every possible last touch had been put on the house that she departed for a grand tour of Europe with her children. During that extended trip, Mrs. Westcott further exhibited her progressive attitude by placing her son in the first Montessori school ever opened. Very fortunately, one of her plans miscarried. Just as the family was about to return home, her son fell ill and the trip had to be deferred to a later date. They had booked passage on the *Titanic*!

In addition to the house itself, Wright added to the design in January 1908, by creating a garage and stables at the end of the lot. These he connected to the house by a walkway, which had an exterior wall on Greenmount Avenue and was topped with an arbor, or trellis-like structure. Foliage was to be placed in planters at intervals along the top of the exterior wall and then vine over the trelliswork, as well as hang down the exterior wall.

Although Frank Lloyd Wright and Louis Sullivan eventually disagreed on some points, one thing they both believed in was a horizontal thrust to buildings. Such was the aim of Sullivan's later designs and it was the pivotal point for Wright's concept of the "Prairie House": a building in harmony with the surface of the ground, especially Midwestern prairies.

The Westcott House and its extension is the complete fulfillment of that idea. Here everything is level and horizontal, each in its own plane, which is parallel with every other line in the house. These planes are then reinforced in the viewer's mind by the use of exterior woodwork that is stained to contrast with the stucco of the body of the house. It can be easily noted on the Greenmount Avenue side how this motif was beautifully executed. A wooden band was brought out from the terrace, allowed to drop to ground level and then connected to a band that runs all the way back to the garage *(see figure 200, page 161)*.

The interior of the house is also a complete statement as to Wright's beliefs. The dining, living and family rooms are all one unit, stretching across the front of the house, each separated from the other by merely a low, divider wall with open top ❊ *(fig. 201, left, at top)*.[13] The effect is highly reminiscent of Wright's beloved Japanese house form.

The Westcott House and its companion Prairie Houses in other areas are today considered the prototypes or forerunners of the modern "ranch" house. Low divider walls, windows ranged in groups within a single, horizontal casement and level design, not to mention rooms flowing into each other without doors, are all derived from these early products of Wright's genius. Yet what we take for granted today were radical innovations as well as departures from tradition in the pre-1910 period. After a few years of growth, the exterior landscaping as well only added to the overall Japanese feeling of the house ❊ *(fig. 202, left, bottom picture)*.

Wright built not another thing in Ohio for the next forty years and no one attempted to duplicate or imitate the Westcott House in Springfield, or Clark County. In 1915, however, Arthur W. Grant built an interesting rectilinear house at 1812 East High Street ❊ *(fig. 203, page 167)*. Grant had been the inventor of a rubber tire and was involved in a number of Springfield businesses, including the Kelly Rubber Tire Company.

[13] *The kitchen and laundry room are completely separate, for they were considered "laboratories" by the architect, and not part of the family living space.*

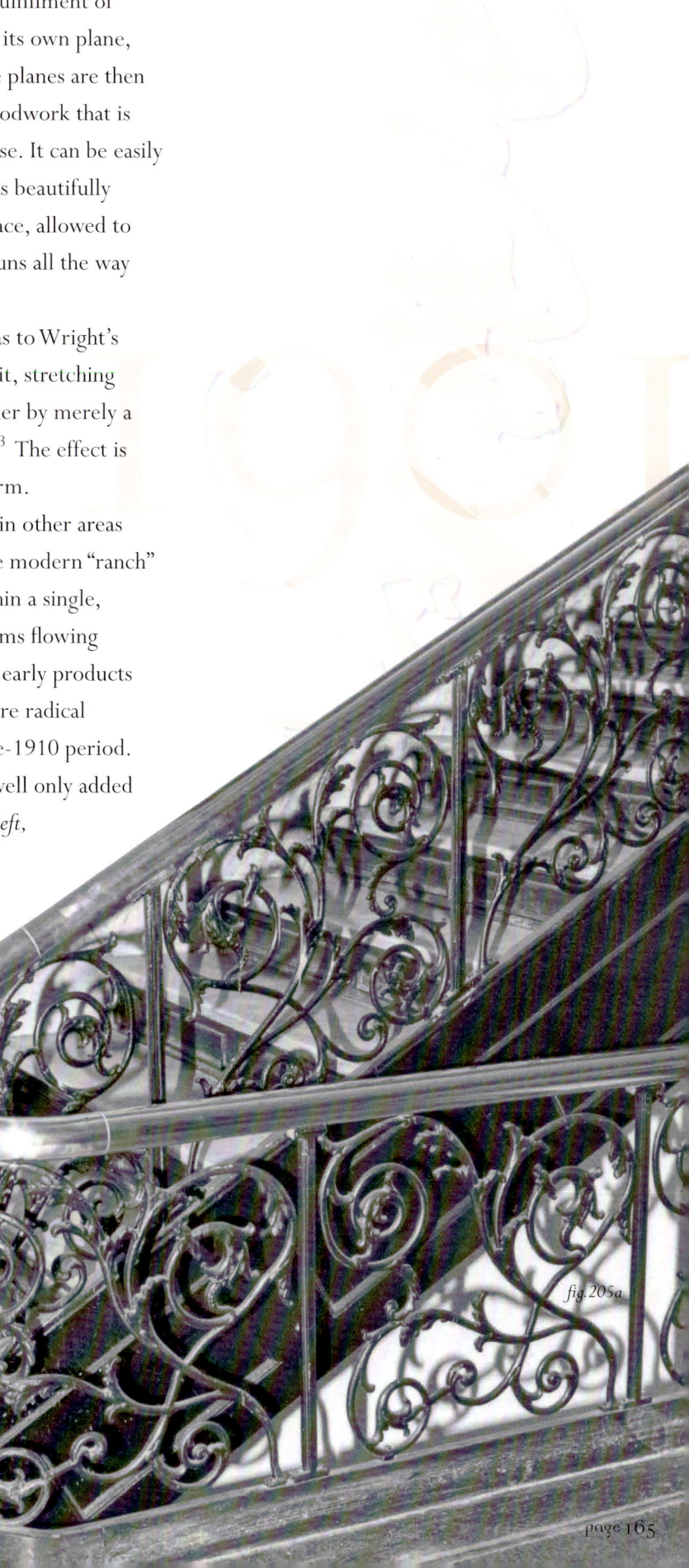

fig. 205a

The house has often been attributed to Wright, but no documentation exists that Wright had any connection with the design whatsoever. The structure is definitely not a Prairie House, but may have been derived indirectly from two other of Wright's buildings.

In 1904 he built the Unity Temple in Chicago, and then in 1911 the Midway Gardens Amusement Center. Both of these feature a rectangular central pavilion with flanking wings. The Unity Temple has overhangs much like the Grant House and Midway Gardens has the pavilion recessed between the wings, also like the Grant House. Thus, Arthur W. Grant's home owed something to Wright, but probably more in the sense of general tendency rather than specific application.

In 1916 Charles Schmidt of the Schmidt & Botley Nursery in Springfield built another rectilinear house. This one is more of a country home and is located on the Yellow Springs Street, just beyond the current city limits *(fig. 204, right, at bottom)*. In overall impact and design, the structure is quite similar to Grant's and represents something of the vanguard of architectural home design of the era. It has been known for some time as the Bethesda Home.

On the whole, however, there was little visible impact upon Springfield domestic architecture from the works of Louis Sullivan and his disciple, Frank Lloyd Wright. Commercial and public design experienced some effects, but again, it was more in the line of a general tendency among architects.

One of the few relics in Springfield that faintly reflects the Sullivan period is the grand staircase in the Clark County Building, now known as the A. B. Graham Building, at Limestone and Columbia Streets. The structure was designed in a strict Beaux Arts Classical Revival mode by Robert Gotwald and erected in 1901. The main staircase, however, was done in a delightful *Art Nouveau* form with an openwork cast-iron balustrade *(fig. 205a, previous page)*. While the actual forms within the ironwork are not quite as abstracted as Sullivan might have done, as in the Carson Pirie Scott & Co. entryway in Chicago *(fig. 205b, page 156)*, still the effect of it against the otherwise severe interior is probably the same as what Sullivan might have sought. The most casual glance around the city and county shows that most residents opted for Classical, Colonial, Georgian or other picturesque revival styles of architecture in the early decades of the century.

Burton J. Westcott and Frank Lloyd Wright both shared one thing in common—unhappiness. Westcott strove hard to be progressive and establish a reputation for integrity. In 1914 he helped establish the City Commission form of government, which promised to eliminate corruption. He was later attacked for it.

In 1916 he began manufacturing the Westcott automobile in Springfield ❋ *(fig. 206, page 161)*, but was forced out of the market by 1925 and sold the company. In 1923 his beloved wife, Orpha, underwent a routine sinus operation in Philadelphia. While recovering she contracted spinal meningitis and died. She was buried from the house on High Street where Burton was to linger for three more years until his own death in 1926.

Having undergone tremendous historical restoration work in recent years, the house now appears much as it did the day the Westcotts first occupied it. There are no horses or automobiles in the stable-garage, but the lily pond has been reconstructed and the second floor porches have been reopened. As a visitor, you may now walk through the unfurnished rooms, waiting, as it were, for the moving men to bring in the Westcotts' furniture. The house is a monument to Burton and Orpha Westcott, as much as to Frank Lloyd Wright ❋ *(fig. 207, pgs. 162–163)*.

fig. 203

203 (above). The Arthur W. Grant House, 1812 East High Street, as it appeared in 1927, after being sold to H. J. Fahien. From Artwork of Springfield, 1927.
204 (below). The Charles Schmidt House, Yellow Springs Street, south of city limits. Schmidt was partner with Robert H. Botley, first as florists and later as nurserymen.

204 *The Charles Schmidt House, Yellow Springs Street, south of city limits.*

Harry S. Kissell

One of the greatest of the Springfield entrepreneurs, Harry S. Kissell, was born here September 24, 1875, the son of Cyrus and Lucretia Kissell, and a descendant of one George Kissell, a Pennsylvania farmer. George's own grandfather, Nicholas Kissell, had been one of the Moravian founders of Lietz, Pennsylvania, in 1718. After several more moves and false starts, Harry Kissell's grandfather, Emmanuel, arrived in Springfield in 1851.

Although Emmanuel Kissell never seemed to find the career that precisely suited him, his son Cyrus easily and quickly found his niche in life. In an era when buying a home with a mortgage was tremendously difficult for the average man, Kissell determined to make it easier.

In 1884 he opened a real estate and loans office in Springfield. His philosophy of community stability based on widespread home ownership, financed by reasonable loans, caused the firm to prosper. By the 1890s his son, Harry, was ready to join the business.

Three years after his father's death in 1903, Harry Kissell incorporated the Kissell Real Estate Company with capital stock of $10,000. This began his career, which lasted until 1946 and included the presidency of The Fairbanks Building Co., and directorships of both the American Trust & Savings and First National Banks. One of his early and major accomplishments, of course, was development of the Ridgewood addition to Springfield.

HARRY S. KISSELL
President and Treasurer The Kissell Real Estate Company
Director The American Trust and Savings Company

Kissell also had a far-reaching influence in the mechanics of real estate. He organized the National Association of Real Estate Boards and then joined in the development of the National Home Loan Bank. Both creations helped promote real estate purchases in an era with no readily available loan funds.

In 1934, Kissell helped the passage of legislation that eventually created both the Federal Housing Administration and the Federal Savings and Loan Insurance Corporation. The result: organizations providing both money for the purchase of homes and safe places to keep hard-earned income.

Early in 1914, at his suggestion, thirteen local businessmen met to discuss forming a local Rotary Club. The local chapter, with twenty-five members, was quickly formalized and by July membership had increased to forty-one.

When Harry Kissell died in 1946, his firm bore small resemblance to that of his father's. Today's mortgage companies, in turn, seem radically unlike what they were in Harry's lifetime. Nevertheless, Cyrus's—and then Harry's—basic philosophy still prevails: "The key to a stable community is property ownership."

A caricature of Harry S. Kissell (at left) that originally appeared in the 1907 publication Springfield Men of Affairs. Kissell was instrumental in the construction of the Fairbanks Building (at right), later the First National Bank Building, which had the distinction of being the city's first skyscraper when it was built in 1905. Still standing at 4 W. Main St., the office building originally housed a variety of tenants, including the Kissell Real Estate Co. It also boasted a theater on the ground floor.

no place like home | pares cum paribus congregantur

SUITS & O-COATS
MILLARDS
ALL $22.50
WHY PAY MORE?
GEIGER
LAW
OCT. 3rd

Bungalo
A FEW MORE

It is the custom with most symphony orchestras to follow their main performance with one or two light pieces of music, at the demand of the audience. Of course, the audience knows it is supposed to demand these *encores*, and the orchestra has already practiced the pieces which will be demanded of it. Nineteenth-century architecture began with the great Greek Revival symphony, continued with a Gothic Revival Divertimento and was followed by an Italianate Intermezzo. The concluding works were a Fantasia on Eastlake-Queen Anne and the magnificent Classical Revival Suite. The first encore was Frank Lloyd Wright; yet the audience demanded more and not quite so *avant-garde*, either.

During the last five years of the 1890s, the *Ladies' Home Journal* began to popularize what was called the bungalow. The word *bungalow* was derived from a dialect in the State of Bengal in India. It referred to a style of lightly built guest houses, which had deep eaves and an extensive veranda *(fig. 208, below)*. Translated to the United States, it became a one-story frame house of a long, rectangular shape with wide eaves and a front porch. The porch was very squarely designed so that it could be easily enclosed, if desired. The essence of the house was its narrowness and cheapness, which made it perfect for the expanding housing market being created all across the country to accommodate an ever-enlarging population *(fig. 209, above, at right)*.

Its initial popularity was found in California, where the mild climate would support flimsy construction. As the design moved eastward, different methods of construction became necessary to make it habitable where the winters could be harsh, including quantities of rain, snow and ice.

Indigenous California and western states architecture had tended from the beginning to be one story in height, especially so in those places where trees were few and lumber sold at a premium. Eastern designs, however, favored the traditional concept of sleeping rooms on a second floor, if only

208 (background screen, below). Early twentieth-century woodcut of typical Bengalese bungalow, as found in original form in India.
209 (above). Bungalow of the simplest form, North Chillicothe Street, South Charleston, Ohio.
211 (left). Bungalow with hipped roof and dormer, Pitchin Road, Springfield Township.

ENCORES

chapter FIFTEEN

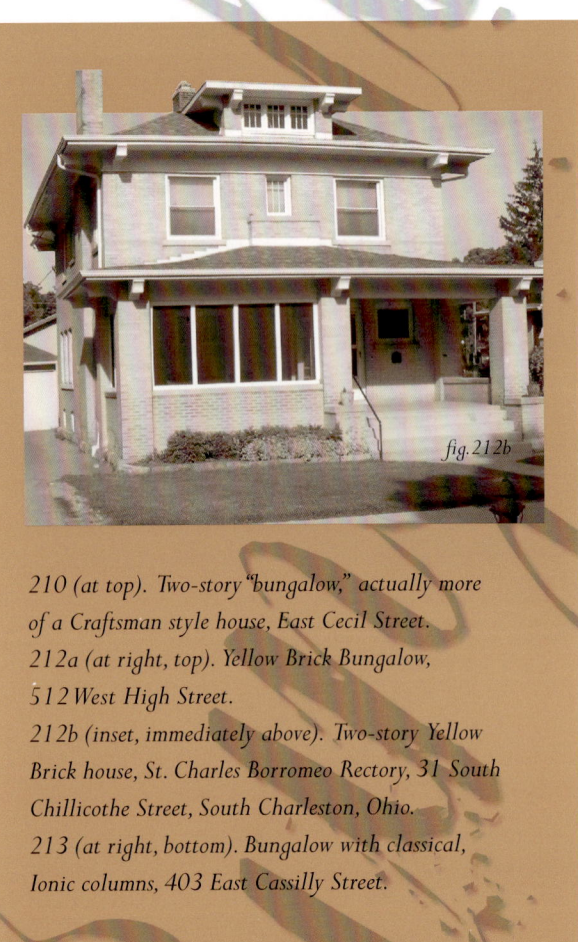

210 Two-story "bungalow" with tiled roof, East Cecil Street.

210 (at top). Two-story "bungalow," actually more of a Craftsman style house, East Cecil Street.
212a (at right, top). Yellow Brick Bungalow, 512 West High Street.
212b (inset, immediately above). Two-story Yellow Brick house, St. Charles Borromeo Rectory, 31 South Chillicothe Street, South Charleston, Ohio.
213 (at right, bottom). Bungalow with classical, Ionic columns, 403 East Cassilly Street.

to allow them to catch a breeze in the summer. Although millions of one-story bungalows were built east of the Mississippi, anyone who has lived in an urban version on its narrow lot—without air conditioning—can tell you of the ghastly heat generated in them in the summer! For this reason, then, where land and money were available, eastern bungalows soon acquired a second story. Where there was no restriction on lot/land size, these homes grew fat and broad, but the deep front porch remained *(fig. 210, above).*

The earliest bungalows usually received a hipped roof; that is, the gable looked as though it had been sliced at an angle backwards from the eaves. With so little space available on the one floor, attic storage was imperative and, to compensate for heat in the summer and allow ventilation, a hipped dormer was commonly constructed above the eaves at the front. On larger versions, dormers facing three different directions might be built *(fig. 211, page 170).*

After the bungalow had met and married the traditional eastern requirements in

212a *Yellow Brick Bungalow, 512 West High Street.*

213 *Bungalow with classical, Ionic columns, 403 East Cassilly Street.*

page 173

214 "Octagon" bungalow, East Main Street.

214 (above). "Octagon" bungalow, East Main Street, now razed.
215 (right). Bungalow with gable end to the side, East Cassilly Street.

housing, it soon evolved into little more than a bland or nondescript version of the Colonial Revival box. Commonly built of frame or brick, but just as often stuccoed frame, it was a stark cube with little detailing. In some cases the prominent Japanese influence provided for roofing in red tiles, (*see figure 210, page 172*), which helped to relieve the blandness. In other instances, colored brick, especially a light creamy yellow, was used for the walls. This supplied the only useful name for this hybrid: the Yellow Brick style (*fig's. 212a, previous page, & 212b, page 172*).

The deep porch was, perhaps, the most, if only, enduring/endearing quality about this

NO PLACE LIKE HOME | A FEW MORE ENCORES

architecture. This depth provided a cool retreat on hot summer days and, if screened, provided a pleasant place for sleeping on hot nights. The porch columns, or supports, did vary somewhat. Most were simple square wood or brick supports, but occasionally a pyramidal pylon would be used. On rare occasions, a slight amount of rectilinear decoration in a different color of brick would be attempted near the tops of the supports, but simplicity was usually the goal. A few of the early bungalows built during the Classical Revival period have the porch supported by short, classical columns made of molded concrete ❂ *(fig. 213, page 173).*

In the purer bungalow form, which is usually found on urban lots of the period 1914–1920, the living room commonly had a three-sided bay window projecting onto the porch ❂ *(fig. 214, at left).* Such homes were often called

215 *Bungalow with gable end to the side, East Cassilly Street.*

219 "California" style bungalow, North Chillicothe Street, South Charleston, Ohio.

219 (above, top). "California" style bungalow, North Chillicothe Street, South Charleston, Ohio. 220 (immediately above). Advertisement for an inexpensive, prefabricated bungalow with "jerkin head" roof, American Magazine, September, 1920.

"Octagon Bungalows," but the name is deceptive and has no relevance to the house as a whole. It refers only to the bay window, which would form an octagon, if its shape were completed.

The first major improvement in the bungalow was the removal of the hipped roof. A low, one-story house does not need a low roof. It merely emphasizes the squatness of the structure and holds heat in the summer. Even before the First World War was over, architects had found a new way to orient the roof. First, a half story was added to the overall height of the structure. The entryway was shifted to the middle of one of the long sides. With the triangular gable end on the short side, the roof rose from the backside, peaked at the middle of the house and then sloped forward at a slightly shallower angle. This allowed the roof to go past the front wall of the house and become also the roof of the front porch *(fig. 215, previous page)*. Viewed from the side, the difference in the height of the two roof edges made the structure asymmetrical and added a certain picturesque quality which it had formerly lacked, and thus made it more appealing.

Now, as an alternative to an attic dormer with gable roof, a shed-like dormer could be created on the front or back *(fig. 216, right, at top)*. This, plus the added half story in the walls and the height of the roof allowed for a second-story bedroom. To some architects, these bungalows of unequal roof height with dormer on the front slope, reminded them of Swiss or Bohemian chalets *(fig. 217, at right)*, which had similar profiles due to being built on hillsides. They increased this effect by adding timber struts to the eaves and allowing some rafter ends to protrude beyond the walls. Reorienting the entry to the long side also not only helped to enliven the overall appearance, but also helped to provide a new name for the house. It was now a "California Bungalow" *(fig's. 218, background screen, & 219, left, top)*.

In short, anything was tried to avoid the bland, uninteresting exterior of the average bungalow. One of the more satisfying solutions, especially in the larger form, was to adopt the English "jerkin head" roof which had been employed in the Eastlake period.

This, too, involved using a gable across the house. Unlike the hipped roof, only the two end peaks were cut back. The change was not a radical one, but it did remind people of other places and other times, while giving overall a more pleasing *balance* to the house *(fig. 220, at left, bottom)*. By 1915 there were several prominent national firms that specialized in a whole line of prefabricated bungalows. These were cheap structures often costing less than $1,500, excluding the cost of local work on basement excavation and foundations.

fig. 216

216 (above). Lithograph of a Swiss style chalet, from Holly's Country Seats, by H. H. Holly, 1866.
217 (below). Bungalow with asymmetrical gable and eaves struts; old Route 70, Harmony Township.
218 (background screen, above). Advertisement for a prefabricated "California" bungalow, from, American Magazine, July, 1920.

217 Bungalow, old Route 70, Harmony Township.

page 177

Ridgewood—"in the country club district"

As late as 1908, biographical and historical works on Springfield stated that there were fine residences in the area platted by William and Gustavus Foos, or that someone had an elegant residence on South Fountain Avenue. But, little or nothing was said to truly discriminate one area of the city from another. All of this began to change about 1914.

In 1906, Robert H. Foos, member of a pioneer family of Springfield, helped organize The Springfield Country Club. Foos was already a member of the downtown Lagonda Club, the only English type men's club in the city. Although the club had been in existence for a mere twelve years, it was already old-fashioned by twentieth-century standards. The country club and the Scottish game of golf were the new trend-setting fashion, and it was fashionable to belong and play.

At the same time, real estate developers had begun to widen their vision. Instead of merely buying a piece of land adjacent to or within the city, dividing that into a grid and selling lots, they resurrected an old idea: Llewellyn Park.

Starting about 1862, New York merchant L. S. Haskell began the development at West Orange, New Jersey, of what was the first planned community in the United States. Perhaps spurred by the development of Central Park in New York City, he envisioned an area which, according to landscape designer and horticulturist H. W. Sargent in 1865, would be of an overall higher quality than what was normal at the time. This would be accomplished by maintaining the rural nature of the site through avoidance of rectangular lots, with mutual reference to other properties, the absence of inferior buildings and the development of a suitable approach road and pleasure drives.

Harry S. Kissell, descendant of a long line of Kissells going back into colonial Pennsylvania history, inherited the mantle of real estate development from his father, Cyrus B. Kissell. With a canny eye to possibilities, Kissell surveyed the Springfield scene and noted some interesting facts. One: the new Springfield Country Club was a going concern and likely to grow. It was fashionable and that was where the money was. Two: it lay about a mile north of the developed residential streets on either side of North Fountain Avenue. In that area there was a large amount of undeveloped land.

By 1915 the Kissell Improvement Company was in existence and had acquired about 125 acres of land. It had also met Sargent's concern about the approach—a new entrance road was in place, with Fountain Avenue extended as a boulevard having a center parkway. Being on ground higher than the rest of Springfield and somewhat wooded, the new addition to the city became "Ridgewood."

Within ten years about 50 percent of the lots had been sold and were developed. Much of the rest were sold and only awaiting improvement. After all, as the Kissell Company literature repeatedly stated, these lots were "In the Country Club District." By 1922, even a private school had been built in the area.

The architecture of Ridgewood was varied. Begun just before and reaching its stride during the 1920s, there was a good sprinkling of Mediterranean style homes. Yet the majority of the specimens tended to be Colonial or Georgian revivals, with an English Cotswold or other

RIDGEWOOD

vernacular thrown in for good measure. And here and there a beautiful Adamesque house peeked out from among the soon-to-be unfortunate American Elm trees, with which the area was heavily planted.

While the lots in Ridgewood were never as large as those in Llewellyn Park and there were no pleasure drives, other than the streets themselves, all of the other ideas were implemented. Haskell's concept of winding streets with abundant tree and shrub plantings to simulate a somewhat rural existence was fully met.

Even a major city park designer from Cleveland had been employed to lay out the development. Ridgewood also employed the concept of an annual assessment on lot holders for maintenance of the area.

Despite a semirural ambience the Kissell Improvement Co. was quick to point out that every lot was supplied with natural gas and electricity, all streets were paved and lighted, and there was abundant street car transportation to the inner city. Although no one said it, East High Street and South Fountain Avenue were now matters of history. By 1924, so, too, was the Victorian concept of the gentleman's refuge—the Lagonda Club. It now housed the Chamber of Commerce and everyone was welcome there for lunch in the basement dining room.

At bottom left— From the cover of a promotional booklet, which was issued by The Kissell Improvement Company that touted the amenities and advantages of Springfield's first "planned" residential community. At left, background screen—A 1920s map advertises the lots that are still available in the Ridgewood subdivision. Immediately below—the country club. At bottom—Harry S. Kissell, pictured third from the left, walks next to Theodore Roosevelt during the President's visit to Springfield in 1917.

page 179

Eclectic

AND STILL MO

While the average man who was seeking a new home ran into a solid line of bungalows, "Yellow Brick" and "Colonial Revival" boxes, persons of wealth continued to play the game of revivalism. Hard on the heels of Colonial-Georgian mansions and Genoese palazzos came a renewed interest in English Tudor architecture. It became a passion among architects and clients to see who could design the most archaeologically correct masterpiece. Even Frank Lloyd Wright was not immune to the disease. In 1894 he had accepted a commission for a Tudor style mansion in Oak Park, Illinois. When that house burned in 1922, he replaced it with another!

What was called "Tudor," however, was in reality a medley of different English tidbits thrown together. Ideally it should have been a brick or stone house, two or more stories high, with a gable roof. There should be at least one gabled crossing wing and at least one bay rising the full height of the house. The chimneys should be soaring and topped with chimney pots. What emerged from drafting boards was often radically different (fig. 221, below, right).

To avoid the "coldness" of dressed stone, brickwork was often substituted. This was acceptable, but a wing in a half-timbered style was often appended. But half-timbering was a Mediaeval trait, not a true Tudor one (fig. 222, below). Figure 223 (above, right) shows a Warwickshire, England, half-timbered house in 1889. It illustrates well the building method, which utilized bricks as filling

221 (below). Woodcut of Sir Walter Raleigh's Tudor style residence at Youghal, Ireland, National Magazine, July, 1856.
222 (screen, near left). Woodcut of the half-timbered style home of the English poet Cowley, in Surrey County; pre-seventeenth century. March, 1853.
223 (above). Half-timbered house in Warwickshire, England, photographed in 1889. Poorly maintained, the brick fill under the exterior plaster is clearly visible.
224 (far left). The Harry S. Kissell House, 1801 North Fountain Boulevard, contemporary photograph.

MORE ENCORES

chapter SIXTEEN

226 *The Deer-Kuss House, 1909 Walnut Terrace, designed in a revival of the Adamesque style.*

fig. 225

no place like home | and still more encores

between upright timbers. As can be seen, plaster was usually applied over the bricks. The technique continued to be used in the Tudor period, but principally for more humble homes and shops, not great mansions. The modern creation of a combination of styles could only be justified as an academic example of a Mediaeval house that had received a new addition at a later period.

There was, of course, nothing wrong with a house of this type. They were large, spacious, comfortable and, above all, picturesque, even if they were out of their time period. Such homes, which were expensive, were commonly built by men in the banking and stockbrokering professions. As a result, some critics sneered and called them "Stockbroker Tudor." Yet, it gave the owner a feeling of security and "roots."

Whether the criticism was merited is now almost immaterial. The style found great acceptance and was utilized across the United States. It became truly popular in Springfield about the end of World War I, although there is some true Tudor style brickwork at the third-floor level of the Lagonda Club Building, of 1894–1895, by Frank Andrews. The Harry Kissell House (fig. 224, page 180) is perhaps the most prestigious example of the style, but there were many others (fig. 225, at left, bottom).

At the same time that the ersatz Tudors were coming into favor, the Colonial Revival changed course. The public began to develop a renewed interest in the style of the Brothers Adam. This, of course, was a type of eighteenth-century Neoclassical, but much more severe than the usual Georgian idiom. Adamesque town houses were usually built of dark red brick, relieved here or there with light stone dressings, particularly keystones above the windows and a small classical portico over the door (fig. 226, left, above). The Adam interest was combined with the general outline of the Renaissance palace, which had been built by the wealthy since the early 1890s, with a trace of Wright's rectilinear influence added for good measure.

By 1918 another encore in eclecticism had been produced: New Neoclassic, or Neo-Neoclassical! This form of house was a two-story, rectangular box, sometimes with a base almost imperceptibly larger than the top. The entryway was recessed within the exterior walls, with two stone columns supporting a single arch of brick or stone.

The windows were treated as Wright would have done: they were banked in groups of three at least, within a single casement. The roofs were low and hipped, while the chimneys were grouped together with a flat stone cap, much again in Wright's manner (fig. 227, near left). Lacking the extensive detail work of the true Renaissance palace, the house could

225 (left). The H.V. Bretney House, 1602 North Fountain Boulevard; a highly eclectic design featuring Tudor effect in gables, Neoclassical entryway, and rectilinear influence in window treatments, built ca. 1917. 227 (below). The Pazzi Chapel, Florence, Italy. This Renaissance entryway was revived in "Neo-Neoclassical" homes in the early twentieth century.

page 183

228a (right, top). The Eakins House, North Fountain Boulevard, now razed. 228b (right, bottom). The F. S. Hunting House, 918 North Fountain Avenue; an even more spectacular rectilinear house than the Eakins home. 229 (below). Advertisement for a Mission style table; Leslie's Monthly Magazine, February, 1905.

be expanded or contracted according to one's means. At the time of its popularity, Fountain Boulevard was being developed as a new residential area. It and many of its adjacent side streets received a number of these Neo-Neoclassic homes in a variety of sizes, with considerable differences in the treatment of minor details ✦ *(fig's. 228a[14] & b, at right)*.

Due to the use of supporting columns and occasionally an exterior hood over the doorway, these homes were sometimes called "Colonial" in design. Yet the "Colonial" element in them, minimal at best, is their derivation ultimately from the Adam style, which was used in late eighteenth- and early nineteenth-century America.

While the eastern United States was largely preoccupied, architecturally, with Classical and Tudor revivals, as well as bungalows, the West Coast had begun to resurrect its past. California architects began to draw and popularize homes in the "Mission" style. This involved essentially a low one- or two-story structure, stuccoed and painted white on the exterior. There would often be at least one wing in a rectangular shape, with hipped or pyramidal tiled roof and a gallery with low arches reaching almost to the ground. The most notable part would be a section a trifle higher than the rest, with a wavy or stepped-edge parapet of a roughly triangular shape. This represented the "mission church" part of the ensemble and the niche was the empty belfry. The several expositions between 1892 and 1918 all helped to popularize the style, culminating in the California-Pacific Exposition of 1915.

The interiors of these homes were commonly finished in a medium dark oak woodwork and usually had a Spanish Colonial fireplace. This latter featured a prominently projecting stone hood with sculptured decoration. The furniture was commonly of a very rectangular nature and popularized by Gustav Stickley. Stickley was a Chicago furniture maker who caught the Mission fever. He produced and popularized this rectangular style of furniture, supposedly based on the crude pieces built for the early California missions by the Indian convert-workers. In fact, the whole Mission Period produced a new wave of interest and intensity in the Arts and Crafts Movement ✦ *(fig. 229, at left)*.

The chief prophet of Arts and Crafts was Elbert Hubbard. In 1895 he settled at East Aurora, New York, where he established a colony of artists and artisans called the "Roycrofters." From here, for the next twenty years, he blasted conventional society through the pages of his magazine, *The Philistine*, and promoted the Mission School-Stickley attitude towards

---

[14] *This home, the H. Eakins House, on Fountain Boulevard, was demolished in recent years.*

228a The Eakins House, North Fountain Boulevard, now razed.

228b The F. S. Hunting House, 918 North Fountain Avenue.

page 185

231b The older section of Springview Sanitarium, now a Clark County Building.

the arts and crafts, including furniture. Today Hubbard is remembered chiefly for his Spanish-American War essay, "A Message to Garcia." He was traveling to Europe aboard the liner *Lusitania*, when it was torpedoed off Ireland on May 7, 1915. He and his wife both drowned; so also did the Mission style.

To judge from the homes still standing in Springfield and Clark County, the Mission style found little favor here on the whole, and virtually none in homes. The closest we can come to anything in that mode—and it is not very close—is the former C. I. Weaver House on East High Street, now demolished (fig. 230, at right). Here the architect created a true hybrid. The basic shape of the structure was that of the Renaissance rectangular cube with recessed entryway. The windows were done in casements, *a la* Wright, but the chimneys were at the ends, rather than the middle. The whole exterior was stuccoed in proper Mission style, and projecting timbers supported window and door hoods, but in no particular fashion.

The interior was done in "Mission Oak" and had a dramatic Spanish fireplace in the living room. The Spanish interior and the exterior stuccoing, plus the lack of ornamentation, gave it the major Mission characteristics, but its rectilinear lines make it a definite product of eastern United States architectural thought.

What is lacking in local domestic architecture can be illustrated by two other pieces of architecture, one commercial and one civil. The façade of the Springfield Engraving Company on Roosevelt Drive presents a highly stylized version of Mission architecture. A touch of quaintness is supplied

230 (above). The C. I. Weaver House, East High Street, ca. 1913, now razed. 231a (below). The Springfield Engraving Company, with Mission style façade, Roosevelt Drive. 231b (at left). The older section of Springview Sanitarium, now a Clark County Building, on the eastern limits of Springfield, in the Mission style.

231a The Springfield Engraving Company, Roosevelt Drive.

page 187

234 (above, left). Romanticized nineteenth-century version of an English Cotswold Cottage, National Magazine, 1856.
235 (above, right). A modern Cotswold Cottage, of modest size and dimensions, 205 Ardmore Road.

by the purposely unstuccoed bricks here and there that represent the aged, chipped walls of a California mission (*fig. 231a, previous page*). An academically more satisfying specimen is the older wing of the Springview Sanitarium on the eastern limits of the city (*fig. 231b, page 186*).

In the midst of the Mission Period, Stickley's style of furniture began to affect architecture. What evolved was a cross between the ultra plain bungalow, the two-story Yellow Brick and the existing Mission style. Stickley published a magazine called *The Craftsman*, and it was this that lent its name to the new hybrid.

Craftsman style houses exist by the thousands in Springfield and other communities. They were easy to build, being a square cube with virtually no exterior decoration, although they routinely did have a comfortable front porch. Occasionally the very best models had imitation Colonial rafters under the broad eaves. They were most commonly built of horizontal wooden siding, although brick specimens are not unusual.

The roof was normally of the hipped variety, covered with slates in the more expensive models. Attics often had at least one dormer, gable or shed variety, to ventilate the excessive summer heat, especially in the Midwest.

Perhaps the most distinctive feature of these homes was the low divider that separated the entryway or foyer from the living room. This low wall terminated in a wooden column that reached to the ceiling. This and other interior woodwork and doors was commonly stained and varnished. Housekeeping customs of the period dictated that woodwork should be revarnished each spring. The end result was a gradually darkening interior. Later attempts to reverse this by overpainting in some light color usually resulted in disastrous *alligatoring* of the paint surface.

The Craftsman style house served a very definite function. It provided durable and respectable housing, without frills, to an ever-expanding middle class ready to become homeowners. It leaves everything to be desired in an architectural style.

The bungalow craze is generally credited with reaching its peak about 1914–1920, yet, long before that, other smaller house styles began to appear. One of the most popular—and there were a number of them in Springfield by 1914—was a revival of the so-called "Dutch Colonial." The style was devised by Dutch and German settlers in seventeenth-century Pennsylvania, and then spread to New York and the New England states. It consisted of a rectangular house, often with recessed entryway on the long wall, topped by a gambrel roof.

The gambrel is much like a mansard, in that it rises from the eaves at a steep angle, and then, at about two-thirds the height of the roof, the pitch changes to a very shallow angle. Unlike the mansard, the gambrel rises from only two sides of the house, the long sides. The other two have the walls carried up to the ridge of the roof. Very commonly gable or shed dormers project from the lower section of the gambrel. Also, unlike the mansard, the bottom edge of the gambrel is allowed to extend out beyond the house wall, so as to afford some protection from rain to anyone standing at the door.

The chimney is usually at one or both ends, although the English settlers often moved the chimney to the center of the house to conserve heat. Most Dutch Colonials are built of frame, but some appeared in brick, stucco or even stone. Two of the best examples, probably designed by the same architect, are at 412 East High Street (fig. 232, top, right), and at the corner of Fountain and McCreight Avenues. The style is occasionally still being built today.

With the conclusion of the First World War in 1918 and

232 (above). Dutch Colonial house, 412 East High Street. The enclosed porch at the west end is probably a semimodern remodeling.
233 (below). "Garrison Colonial" as seen in the famous Allyn House; seventeenth century, Massachusetts. Notice the Mediaeval style overhang. Compare with illustration fig. 150 (page 118). This design was often revived in twentieth-century architecture.

1920

236 (below). The Ponce de Leon Hotel, St. Augustine, Florida, as it appeared in 1896.
237a (above). The John L. Bushnell mansion, 2110 East High Street, built 1920–21.

the ensuing eleven years of rampant prosperity, Americans increasingly shook off the starkness of the bungalow era and began searching for something more picturesque in housing for the average man. For those of a purely American bent, all manner of Colonial styles were revived, in addition to the already-existing Dutch Colonial. The Cape Cod Colonial of one and one-half stories and simple design, rectangular box with gable roof and scant exterior ornamentation, was perfect for mass housing. It remained so up through the 1950s and can be seen today by the thousands in early suburban developments.

Somewhat more picturesque was the Cape Ann Colonial, a smaller version of the Dutch Colonial, also with a gambrel roof. Equally quaint was "Garrison Colonial," patterned after sixteenth-century New England homes with overhang, which themselves had been modeled on Mediaeval English styles *(fig. 233, previous page)*. The list of variants is almost interminable. Many of these designs and adaptations were given the name of bungalow, apparently to account for their size and one-floor plan.

For those seeking a European flavor or greater quaintness, architects seized upon the smallest of the English designs, the Cotswold Cottage. This form of house had apparently been introduced into England about the time of the Norman Conquest in 1066 and continued in use up through the Elizabethan period. The basic shape was a rectangle with gable or jerkinhead roof. Perpendicular to the body of the house was a short addition with a pointed gable and massive fireplace chimney attached to the exterior. There could even be a smaller gable addition in front of that containing the actual front door. The eaves of the roof and any dormers usually had rounded edges, in imitation of the thatching used on original models in England.

The several sections being of different sizes and grouped irregularly, the total effect was highly picturesque *(fig. 234, page 188)*. Since the originals were constructed in a casual fashion with any building materials handy, these revival forms often had brick, half-timbering and even fieldstone combined *(fig. 235, page 188)*.

The last of the great revival styles of architecture originated in Florida. From the 1880s onward, persons of means had been traveling south in the winter to avoid the northern snows. Financier and railroad entrepreneur Henry Flagler had catered to these people by gradually pushing his Seaboard Airline Railroad south, ultimately terminating at Key West. The earlier terminus at St. Augustine had not only brought an influx of tourists, but also the buildings to house them. Given the warm climate of Florida, late nineteenth-century architects had sought a style that would be suitable and had settled on a kind of grandiose Neo-Moorish for luxurious tourist hotels such as the Ponce de Leon (fig. 236, bottom, left). By the early 1920s, the wealthy were flocking to Palm Beach or Miami, and a land boom was in full swing.

The official style of Florida architecture was finally settled in those days by Addison Mizner at Palm Beach. Mizner had studied in Spain at the University of Salamanca and was just as entranced by the local architecture as Richardson had been with that of Provencal France. He arrived in Palm Beach in 1918 and almost immediately began a career of designing fantastic mansions in an eclectic style combining Spanish, Spanish Colonial, and general Mediterranean elements, but especially Moorish. A similar theme was carried out at Coral Gables by architect George Merrick.

Although the results in each case varied, Mizner's homes all had certain traits in common. They were two- and three-story buildings, slightly widening toward the ground. The roofs were hipped and covered with red Spanish tiles. Windows were frequently tall and arched and grouped into pairs, with the divider being a stone column. Most of these houses had either an interior courtyard, or a rear garden, which was entered from the house through an arched gallery. Unlike California arches, these were much taller and carried on stone columns rather than stuccoed brickwork. Doorways frequently had elaborate wrought-iron grills of Spanish motif.

Inasmuch as both California and Florida had initially been explored and settled by the Spanish, the Mission style had initially seemed the logical choice for Florida architecture. But the clients who had truly outstanding pieces of architecture commissioned, however, were of such wealth and social station that the size and informality of the Mission style was inappropriate. The choice, therefore, of a Hispano-Moorish style in a general Renaissance form of greater formality was inevitable. The skyrocketing popularity and influence of Hollywood, the motion picture industry and, above all, the Latin star Rudolph Valentino, only confirmed this desire for Mediterranean architecture. Further to the north, where the social scene required even greater formality, those of means once again adopted a pure Italian Renaissance movement.

Springfield felt the effect of both movements. Although a number of homes were built on Fountain Boulevard and elsewhere with the general lines of this Italo-Hispanic style, only three houses qualify as true

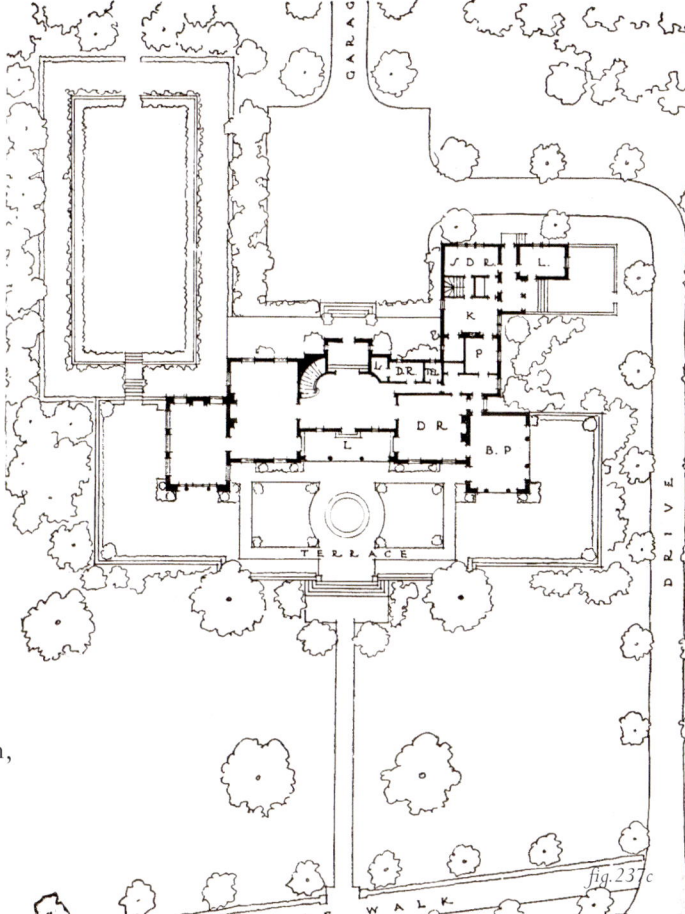

237b (below). Detail of the arcaded entrance to the John Bushnell mansion. 237c (above). Blueprint of the John Bushnell mansion.

238 *The Charles I. Shawyer House, 101 Brighton Road, built 1921–22 in the Mediterranean style.*

no place like home | and still more encores

representatives. In 1920–1921, JOHN L. BUSHNELL, son of former Governor Asa S. Bushnell, erected an elegant home at 2110 East High Street. The structure was in the Italian Renaissance mode with a delightful three-bay arcade facing High Street and a glassed-in side porch having a doorway reminiscent of Mizner's best design work ✺ *(fig's. 237a, page 190; 237b & c, page 191)*. In more recent times it was razed to make way for a high-rise apartment house known as Governor's Manor. Needless to say, the name of the apartment house is a misnomer, since Governor Asa Bushnell had been dead for seventeen years when the house was built! The small strip mall on East Main Street, behind the property, does better, being called simply "Bushnell Plaza."

About a year later, in 1921–1922, CHARLES I. SHAWYER erected a large home ✺ *(fig. 238, at left)* in the then-new development of Ridgewood. The Shawyer house has some similarities to the Bushnell mansion, but is lacking in much of the detail work. The most notable omission, of course, is the elegant arcaded entryway that made the John Bushnell mansion so typical of the Florida movement. Then, in 1924–1925, Arthur E. Jones built a home at 1821 North Fountain Boulevard ✺ *(fig. 239, page 195)* that was something of a scaled-down version of the Florida style. The house also has quite a bit of California influence and may rightly be termed "Mediterranean," as some have called such hybrids.

The most grandiloquent statement of the Florida style in Springfield is the mansion built by C. F. GREINER, Vice-President of the Buffalo-Springfield Roller Company, in 1926. When the house was conceived, the family already had a Florida connection. Charles M. Greiner, president of the company and father of C. F., was semiretired and a resident of Sea Breeze, and later Daytona Beach, Florida.

The house ✺ *(fig. 240, next page)* was built just beyond the eastern city limit, off Route 41 at the top of a hill. In the best Italian tradition, the structure sits upon an artificial terrace faced with smoothly dressed stone. The terrace itself is enclosed with a railing of classically shaped balusters, from which two stone staircases descend to the garden level. Between the staircases is a lemonhead fountain that spouted water into a shallow basin.

The main block of the house rises two stories from the terrace, culminating in a low, hipped tile roof. On the garden side, the entrance is through a seven-bay arcade, the arches of which are carried on stone columns. Although now enclosed, the arcade was originally open, with greater effect. At either end of the terrace wrought-iron lanterns were hung from horseshoe arches having a general Mediterranean motif. Also, in

1927

the best Italian tradition, the house has a main block plus lesser appendages. Such villas in Italy often received various additions over the centuries, which spoiled their symmetry but added to their picturesque quality.

The body of the house was stuccoed, but seems originally to have been painted a shade close to the stonework terrace, rather than the brilliant Florida white, so popular for stucco then and now. The whole ensemble was a brilliant architectural *tour de force* and highly reminiscent of the Villa d'Este at Tivoli, among many others in Italy. This was the last encore.

The building of the Greiner mansion is not the end of the story of Springfield architecture, but it is the end of this volume. From this point onward in time, Springfield, as well as national architecture, follows two different paths. The one path is that of continuing innovation. Many of the designs of the 1930s and 1940s are only now being appreciated and will require at least another generation of study before being properly evaluated. The other path is that of continued repetition. Little can be said of the same "Colonial," tri-level, or ranch house design being used over and over again, often with less and less detail and originality.

What can be said, as a closing remark, is this—nineteenth-century homes, whether excellent, good, bad, or indifferent, have suddenly begun to receive a notice and affection they have not enjoyed since the day they were built. At the same time, revivals of all types of Colonial designs continue to this day. Both phenomena tell us that people basically love an architecture in which they can see something of themselves, or with which they can "identify." We can only wonder how much of the human being there is in bare concrete and exposed steel beams.

Yet, there is hope. When this writing was first completed in 1978, a new Dutch Colonial with gambrel roof had just been built near South Charleston. Now, nearly thirty years later, a massive new Georgian-Colonial Homestead has been built on the other side of the town. We are anxiously awaiting the next wave of French Mansards to sweep the area!

240 *C. F. Greiner House, East High Street.*

239 (below). The Arthur Jones House, 1821 North Fountain Boulevard, built 1924–25.
240 (above). The C. F. Greiner House, East High Street at the city limits, as it appeared soon after construction, from Artwork of Springfield, 1927.

239 *The Arthur Jones House, 1821 North Fountain Boulevard.*

page 195

no place like home

Bibliography

Art Work of Springfield, Ohio: Published in Nine Parts. Chicago: The Gravure Illustration Co., [1927].

Beecher, Catherine. *A Treatise on Domestic Economy*. New York: Harper & Bros., 1846.

Benjamin, Asher. *The American Builder's Companion*, 6th ed. Charlestown, Mass.: S. Etheridge, 1827.

Caffin, Charles H. *How to Study Architecture*. New York: Dodd, Mead and Company, 1925.

The County of Clark, Ohio, an Imperial Atlas and Art Folio. Richmond, Ind.: Rerick Brothers, [1894].

Downing, Andrew Jackson. *The Architecture of Country Houses*. New York: D. Appleton & Co., 1850.

Downing, Andrew Jackson. *Treatise on the Theory and Practice of Landscape Gardening*. New York: O. Judd & Co., 1849.

Fitch, James Marston. *American Building*, 2nd ed. Boston: Houghton Mifflin, 1966.

Gillion, Edmund V. *Pictorial Archive of Early Illustrations and Views of American Architecture*. New York: Dover Publications, 1969.

Gleason's Pictorial Drawing Room Companion, 1853.

The History of Clark County, Ohio. Chicago: W.H. Beers & Co., [1881].

Holly, H. H. *Holly's Country Seats*. New York: D. Appleton & Co., 1866.

Hutslar, Donald. *The Log Architecture of Ohio*. Athens, O.: Ohio University Press, 1977.

Illustrated Historical Atlas of Clark County, Ohio. Philadelphia: L.H. Everts & Co., [1875].

Jackson, Amos Richard. *The Village Builder and Supplement*. New York: A.J. Bicknell, 1873.

LaFever, Minard. *The Modern Builder's Guide*. New York: D. Burgess & Co., 1833.

Maas, John. *The Gingerbread Age*. New York: Bramhall House, 1957.

The New American Primary Speller. Philadelphia: E. H. Butler & Co., [1872].

Palliser's Model Houses. Bridgeport, Conn.: Palliser, Palliser & Company, Architects, [1878].

Reed, S. B. *House Plans for Everybody*. New York: Orange Judd Co., 1878.

Springfield Illustrated, 1889. New York: H.R. Page & Co., [1889].

A Standard History of Springfield and Clark County, Ohio. Chicago: American Historical Society, [1922].

20th Century History of Springfield and Clark County, Ohio: and Representative Citizens. Chicago: Biographical Publishing Co., [1908].

Vaux, Calvert. *Villas and Cottages*. New York: Harper & Bros., 1864.

Wheeler, Gervase. *Rural Homes*. New York: C. Scribner, 1853.

Winter, Gordon. *A Country Camera, 1844-1914*. Baltimore: Penguin, 1973.

Woodward, George E. *Woodward's Cottages and Farm Houses*. New York: G.E. Woodward, 1867.

Woodward, George E. and F.W. Woodward. *Woodward's Country Homes*. 5th ed. New York: G.E. & F.W. Woodward, 1866.

Sources of images

Beecher, Catherine. *A Treatise on Domestic Economy*, 1846: Figure 48.

Benjamin, Asher. *The American Builder's Companion*, 6th edition: Figures 19 & 29.

Berkhofer, George H., collection: Figures 1, 5, 13, 14, 18, 35b, 35c, 39a, 39b, 40a, 40b, 57, 64, 81, 82, 90, 91, 92, 96, 99, 103, 125, 153, 160, 164, 169, 192, 194, 208, 212b, 221, 222, 227, 234, & 236.

Bicknell, A.J. *Bicknell's Village Builder and Supplement*, 1878: Figure 138b.

Clark County Historical Society: Figures 2, 3, 4, 7, 11, 15, 17, 20, 21, 24a, 25, 26, 27, 28, 30, 31, 32, 33, 40, 42, 43, 45, 47, 50, 51, 52, 53, 55, 59, 67c, 69a, 69b, 71, 72, 74, 75, 76a, 78, 80, 85, 89a, 89b, 95, 97, 104, 105, 106, 107, 110, 112, 116, 117, 120, 121a, 121b, 122, 124a, 126a, 126c, 135, 136a, 137a, 139b, 146, 148, 149, 150, 154, 155, 157, 159, 162b, 163, 165a, 167, 168a, 171b, 172, 173, 174, 177, 178, 179b, 180, 183b, 185, 186, 187, 188, 190, 193, 195, 197, 198, 199, 200, 201, 202, 203, 204, 205a, 206, 209, 210, 211, 213, 214, 215, 217, 218, 220, 226, 228a, 228b, 229, 230, 231a, 231b, 235, 239, & 240. Pages 178-179.

Cremer, James. Used with permission from the Fairmount Park Commission Archives, Philadelphia, Pennsylvania: Figure 61.

Dallenbach, Tamara K.: Figure 137b.

Downing, Andrew Jackson. *The Architecture of Country Houses*, 1850. Figures 65a, 65b, 65c, 67a, 67b, 68, 70, 79, 83, 84, 87, 88, 93, 101, 102, 141, 143, 151, & 162a.

Downing, Andrew Jackson, editor. *The Horticulturist and Journal of Rural Art and Taste*, 1846-1852: Figures 58 & 179a.

Downing, Andrew Jackson. *Treatise on the Theory and Practice of Landscape Gardening, With Remarks on Rural Architecture*, 1849: Figures 56a, 56b; Edition of 1865 with Supplement, by H.W. Sargent, Figures 60, 62, & 63.

Gillion, Edmund V., Jr. *Pictorial Archive of Early Illustrations and Views of American Architecture*, 1969. Used with permission from Dover Publications, Inc.: Figures 23, 35a, 36, 37, 44a, 44b, & 233.

Glass, Gregory. AGI Photographic Imaging: Figures 24b, 49, 108, 136b, 161, & 168b; page 108.

Gleason's Pictorial Drawing Room Companion, 1853: Figure 132.

Harper's Monthly Magazine, March 1853: Figures 127, 128, & 129.

Hatfield, Roderick J.: Figures 77, 140, 147, & 176; pages 140-141; and the cover photograph.

Historic American Buildings Survey: Figures 175b, 191, & 205b.

Holly, H.H. *Holly's Country Seats*, 1866: Figure 216.

Hutslar, Donald A. *Log Construction in the Ohio Country, 1750-1850*, 1992. Ohio University Press. Images courtesy of the author: Figures 6, 9, & 10.

LaFever, Minard. *The Modern Builder's Guide*, 1833: Figures 41a & 41b.

Landess, John Turner, collection: Figures 16, 98, 123, 126b, 142, 237a, 237b, & 237c. Pages 92, 93, 109, 122, 123, 139, 154, 155, 168, 169.

The New American Primary Speller by E.H. Butler & Co., Philadelphia, 1872: Figures 130, 131 & 134.

The New York Public Library, Astor, Lenox and Tilden Foundations. Print Collection, Miriam and Ira D. Wallach Division of Art, Prints and Photographs: Figure 8.

Oak Park Public Library, Oak Park, IL. Gilman Lane Collection: Figure 207.

Palliser's Model Houses by Palliser, Palliser & Company, Architects, 1878: Figure 144.

The Philadelphia IronWorks Catalog, 1872: Figure 118.

Reed, S.B. *House Plans for Everybody*, 1878: Figures 109 & 119.

Rose, Kevin R.: Figures 12, 156, 166, 196; pages 108-109; & detail pictures in both front and back matter.

Rottenborn, Emily T.: Figures 94 & 158.

Schory, Ken. www.kenschory.com: Figures 34, 46, 54, 73, 76b, 86, 100, 111, 115, 138a, 139a, 145, 165b, 165c, 170, 171a, 175a, 181a, 181b, 182, 183a, 184, 189, 212a, 219, 224, 225, 232, 238.

Vaux, Calvert. *Villas and Cottages*, 1864: Figures 113 & 114.

Warwickshire Photographic Survey Collection. Used with permission from Birmingham Library Services, Central Library, Birmingham, England: Figure 223.

Wheeler, Gervase. *Rural Homes*, 1853: Figures 66 & 152.

Woodward, George E. *Woodward's Cottage and Farm Houses*, 1867: Figure 133b.

Woodward, George E. & F.W. *Woodward's Country Homes*, 1866: Figure 133a.

1019

no place like home

Index

Adam, James (Scottish architect and furniture designer), 29, 183
Adam, Robert (Scottish architect), 22, 29, 30, 32, 160, 183
Adams Residence, Dr. Samuel E., 100
Adler, Dankmar (Chicago architect), 157, 159
Ambler, John (former Treasurer of Springfield and early builder), 19
American Trust & Savings, 168
American or Vertical Renaissance style (*defined*), 85
Andrews, Frank (Dayton architect and designer of the Lagonda Club Building), 183
antae, 34
Antiquities of Athens (by Stuart & Revett), 32
Architectural Record (of 1908), 164
Architecture (by P. Nicholson), 37
Architecture of Country Houses, The (by A. J. Downing), 53, 62, 68
Art Nouveau style of decoration (*defined*), 158
Arts and Crafts Movement, 184
Auditorium Theatre and Hotel (Chicago, designed by Louis Sullivan), 157, 158

Basilica Vicenza (Vicenza, Italy), 70
Bateman-Wildman House, 83
battens, 54
Beaux Arts (*defined*), 145-146
Beckford, William (English novelist for whom Fonthill Abbey was built), 49
Beecher, Catherine E. (U.S. educator and author), 43
belvedere (*defined*), 72
Benjamin, Asher (New England architect), 22, 30
Bethesda Home, 166
Biddle, Nicholas (American financier), 37
Biographical Record of Clark County, Ohio, The, 92
Black's Opera House, 100
Board of Architects (1893 Columbian Exposition in Chicago), 159
Boathouse in Snyder Park, 155
Bonaparte, Louis Napoleon (Napoleon III, French President, then Emperor), 88, 90, 95, 113
Bookwalter House, Francis, 103
Bretney House, H. V., 183
Brewer Log House, Robert, 10-12, 14
Brownstone Row house, 86
Buchwalter House, Luther, 153
Buena Vista Tavern, 21
Bulfinch, Charles (early American architect), 22, 30, 153
bungalow (*defined*), 171-172, 174-177
Burnham, Daniel (American architect and urban planner), 144, 159
Bushnell House, Asa S., 132
Bushnell House, Ellen Ludlow, 85
Bushnell House, John L., 140, 190-191, 193
Bushnell Plaza, 193
Byron, Lord (English poet), 33

California Bungalow (*defined*), 177
California-Pacific Exposition of 1915, 184
campanile (*defined*), 73
Cape Ann Colonial style (*defined*), 190
Cape Cod Colonial style (*defined*), 190
Carpenter Gothic style (*defined*), 73
Carpenter Renaissance style (*defined*), 83
Carson Pirie Scott Co. Building (Chicago department store), 155, 166
Centennial Exposition of 1876 (Philadelphia), 128, 143, 151
Chippendale, Thomas (furniture designer and builder), 49
Citizens Street Railway Co., 92
City Commission, 166
City Hospital, 68
Clark County Sheriff's Residence, 85
Cogswell House, G.W., 119
Colonial Revival (*defined*), 145-146
Columbian Exposition of 1893 (Chicago), 144, 145, 152, 159
Cotswold Cottage (*defined*), 190
Cottage Color Paint Co., 83
cottage ornée (*defined*), 54
Cottage Residences (by A. J. Downing), 53
Crabill House, David, 21
Craftsman style house (*defined*), 188-189
Craftsman, The (magazine published by Gustav Stickley), 188
Cregar, Charles (Springfield architect), 122, 123, 128, 144, 154
Crowell, J.S. (manager of *Farm and Fireside* magazine), 93, 150, 161

Dalzell's Clearing Near Piqua, 7
Davis, A.J. (American architect), 53, 56, 58, 67
Deer-Kuss House (built by Paul & Elizabeth K. Deer and occupied for many years by Richard L. & Barbara Deer Kuss), 182-183
Dibert Residence, George, 72
Dimond House, The, 116
Directory of the City of Springfield (first published 1852), 108
Doane Residence, Methodist Bishop (New Jersey), 77
Donnel House, 14
Donnel, Jonathan (early settler in Bethel Township), 14
Downey House, W.C., 68, 72, 73, 107
Downing, Andrew Jackson (American landscape designer and writer), **51-54**, 58, 62, 67, 68, 70, 77, 114, 118, 126
Dutch Colonial style (*defined*), 189
Dynes House (South Vienna), 70

Eaker, Letitia (South Fountain Avenue developer), 108
Eakins House, H., 184
Eastlake, Charles Locke (Victorian-era English architect and furniture designer), 114, 160
Eastlake style house (*defined*), 114-115, 116, 118
Ecole des Beaux-Arts, 90, 145, 157

eaves return, 43
entablature (defined), 79
Erechtheum, 34, 39
Erter Homestead, 25
Estle Homestead, 21
Eugenie, Empress (Empress of France), 96, 114
Evans House in South Charleston, 42

Fairbanks Building Co., 168
Farm and Fireside magazine, 93
Farnese Palace (Rome, Italy), 70
Federal Housing Administration, 168
Federal Savings and Loan Insurance Corporation, 168
First National Bank, 168
Fisher, Maddox (early Springfield builder), 19
Flagler, Henry (financier and railroad entrepreneur), 190
Florida style *(defined)*, 191
Foos House, John, 83
Foos, John (former Springfield manufacturer), 83, 140
Foos, Robert H. (member of pioneer Springfield family and co-organizer of The Springfield Country Club), 178
Foos, William and Gustavus (brothers, original developers of East High Street in Springfield), 139, 178
Frederick Louis (Prince of Wales who died in 1751), 47
Fuller House, J.C., 21

Gable, truncated or jerkin headed *(defined)*, 115-116
Gambrill, Charles (American architect), 128
Garnier, Charles (French architect, designer of The Paris Opera House), 90
Garrison Colonial style *(defined)*, 190
Gentleman and Cabinet-maker's Director, The (by Thomas Chippendale), 49
Georgian Revival *(defined)*, 145-146
Gillett, Dr. Berkley (former Clark County physician and owner of Star Cottage), 33, 34, 35
Glessner, J.J. (of Warder, Bushnell & Glessner—Springfield client of H.H. Richardson), 131
Goodfellow House, 25
Gothic Revival *(defined)*, 62
Gothic Villa *(defined)*, 56
Gotwald Building, 42
Gotwald, Dr. Luther A. and Mary King (parents of Robert C., architect), 154
Gotwald, Robert C. (Springfield architect), 133, 147, 154, 155, 166
Gould, Jay ("robber baron" financier who enlarged Lyndhurst), 58
Governor's Manor, 193
Graham Building, A.B., 154-155, 166
"Grand Tour," 65
Grant, Arthur W. (Springfield businessman and inventor), 165
Grant House, Arthur W., 165-166
Greek Orthodox Church, 150
Greek War for Independence (its influence on architecture), 32
Greek Revival style: 34, 35, 38

Corinthian *(defined)*, 39-40
Doric style *(defined)*, 34, 38, 39
Ionic style *(defined)*, 34, 38, 39
Greenough, Horatio (American Neoclassical sculptor of *The Greek Slave*), 158
Greenway Academy, 67, 68, 73
Greiner, C.F. (vice-president of the Buffalo-Springfield Roller Company), 193
Greiner House, C.F., 193, 194

Hagan House, Judge, 133
Harbaugh-Rice House, 89
Haskell, L.S. (New York merchant, designer of Llewellyn Park), 178, 179
Haussman, Baron Georges (Prussian engineer who began the modernization of the city of Paris), 95, 97
Hayward House, M.A., 121
Heritage Commission Depot, 10
Heritage Commission of South Charleston, 10
Hertzler House, Daniel (in George Rogers Clark Park), 25
Hints on Household Taste (by Charles Locke Eastlake), 114
History of Ancient Art (by Johann Winckleman), 32
History of Clark County, Ohio (Beers Co.), 19, 139
Homestead Architecture (by Samuel Sloan), 85
Hoppess Home, John, 140
House & Myers home, 151
Hubbard, Elbert (American author and publisher who established the Roycrofters), 184, 187
Huffman House, Jacob, 15, 19, 22
Huffman, Jacob and Catherine (immigrants from Pennsylvania who settled in Bethel Township), 15
Huffman House, Lewis C., 103
Hunt Homestead, 25
Hunt, Richard Morris (nineteenth-century American architect), 90, 145

Italianate style *(defined)*, 66, 67, 72, 73
Italian Renaissance style *(defined)*, 78, 79

Japanese Movement *(defined)*, 151
Jefferson, Thomas (third President of the U.S.), 30, 50-51
Jones House, Arthur E., 193
Jones, Inigo (English architect), 27
Jones-Kenney-Zechman Funeral Home, 100

Kelly Cottage, O.S., 40-41
Kelly House, O. S., 62, 70
Kenton Farm, Simon, 5
King Building, 42
Kinsman House, 90
Kirkpatrick, T.J. (editor of *Farm and Fireside* magazine), 93
Kissell, Cyrus B. (father of Harry, Springfield real estate and loans office owner), 168, 178
Kissell, Harry S. (Springfield entrepreneur), **168**, 178
Kissell House, Harry S., 62, 183

Kissell Improvement Company, 178, 179
Kissell Real Estate Company, 168
Knights of Pythias Home, 88

Ladies' Home Journal, 160, 161, 171
Lagonda Club, 178, 179, 183
lancet windows, 56
Late Federal Vernacular style (*defined*), 12, 14
Latrobe, Benjamin (English architect who completed the U.S. Capitol), 30, 51
Leffel House, Warren C., 103
L'Enfant, Major Pierre Charles (French artist and engineer who designed Washington, D.C.), 96
Lethly, Marley (Springfield architect), 153
Library of St. Mark (Venice, Italy), 70
Linden Hall Academy at New Carlisle, 42
Linn, James A. (vice-president of the Springfield Publishing Co.), 153
Llewellyn Park, 178, 179
Louvre, the (Paris, France), 88, 96
Ludlow, John (Springfield banker-businessman and original owner of "Oakfield"), 58, 139

Mansardic style (*defined*), 96, 97
Mansart, Francois (seventeenth-century French architect), 96
Marshall Field Wholesale Building (Chicago), 157
Martin, Paul C. (Springfield attorney), 150
Massachusetts Institute of Technology, 157
Mast, Phineas P. (Springfield agricultural manufacturer and industrialist)
  first house, 92-93
  second house, 88-89
  third house, 132
Mast & Co., P.P., 92
Mast Buggy Co., P.P., 93
Mast, Crowell & Kirkpatrick, 93
Mast Foos, 93
McBeth, Alexander (first to build a brick home in Clark County), 19
McKim, Charles (American architect), 145
McKim, Mead & White (architectural firm of New York), 144, 145
Merrick, George (architect developer of Coral Gables, Florida), 191
"Message to Garcia, A" (by Elbert Hubbard), 187
Middleton House, Elijah C., 100, 140
Midway Gardens Amusement Center (built by Frank Lloyd Wright), 166
Mission Period, 184, 188
Mission style (*defined*), 184
Mitchell House, Ross, 133, 140, 154
Mitchell-Thomas Hospital, 68
Mizner, Addison (American resort architect), 191, 193
Monticello, 30
Morgan, Helen Bosart (former owner of the Rowley-Bosart House), 119

Morris, Robert (financier of the American Revolution), 96
Mt. Vernon, 30
Museum of Science and Industry, The, 152
Myers Hall (Wittenberg University), 42

National Association of Real Estate Boards, 168
National Home Loan Bank, 168
National road in Springfield, 25
National Trust, The, 58
Nehls House, Dr., 21
Neoclassical approach (defined), 29, 30
Neoclassical, Neoclassical Revival (defined), 145-146
"New England Farmhouse" (exhibit at Centennial Exposition of 1876), 143
New Neoclassic, or Neo-Neoclassical style (defined), 183, 184
Nicholson, P. (British architect), 37
Notman, John (American architect born in Scotland), 77

Octagon Bungalows (*defined*), 175-176
Ohio History, 161
Ohio log cabin (earliest form), 3, 5
Ohio log cabin (Phase Two), 5, 6, 7
Ohio log house (Phase Three) 9, 10, 11, 12
Osborne House (designed by Prince Albert for Queen Victoria), 67

Palladian (form of Renaissance style, defined), 27, 128
Palladio, Andrea (Italian Renaissance architect), 70, 128
Paris Opera House (Paris, France), 88, 90, 96
Parthenon, 34
Paulding, William (Tarrytown, NY, resident who commissioned A. J. Davis to build Lyndhurst), 58
Peet Co., T.B., 122
Penfield House, 83
Pennsylvania Bank style (*defined*), 23
Pennsylvania House, 92
Pennsylvania style (*defined*), 21, 22
Peoples Federal Savings and Loan Association Building (Sidney, Ohio), 159
Phelps House, Charles (on Ferncliff Place), 128, 133
Philistine, The (Elbert Hubbard's magazine), 184
Phillips mansion, 140
pilasters, 34
Plimoth Plantation in New England, 5
Ponce de Leon Hotel (Florida), 191
"Porch of the Maidens", 34
Prairie Houses (*defined*), 161
Pringle-Patric mansion, 140
Provoost, D.B. (American architect), 103

Queen Anne (former queen of Great Britain), 125
Queen Anne style (*defined*), 126, 127
quoins (defined), 78

Raup Home, Mrs. Gustavus, 153
Recitation Hall (at Wittenberg University), 128

Reid farm, James, 43
Richardson, Henry Hobson, (nineteenth-century American architect), 40, 90, 107, 116, 128, 131, 132, 133, 137, 138, 143, 144, 145, 157, 158, 191
Richardsonian Romanesque style (defined), 131, 132
Ridgewood, 178, 179
Rinehart-Bowman House, 83
Rinehart, John W. (part-owner of Rinehart-Ballard Co.), 83
Robertson, Robert H. (architect who designed the Gov. Asa S. Bushnell mansion), 132, 144
Robinson House (home of the late Virginia Robinson), 83
Robbins, Chandler (founder of Greenway Academy), 67
Rococo furniture style (Louis XIV and Louis XVI revivals, *defined*), 114
Rogers House, Robert, 147
Ross, William (early Springfield builder), 19
Rotary Club, first Springfield, 168
Rowley-Bosart House, 119
Rural Essays (by A. J. Downing), 53
Ruskin, John (English art critic), 128
Russell residence, S., 40 (famous Connecticut residence)

Sargent, H.W. (landscape designer and horticulturist), 178
Schmidt, Charles (part-owner of Schmidt & Botley Nursery in Springfield), 166
Scott, W. A. House, 115
Seaboard Airline Railroad, 190
Second Empire style (See *Mansardic style*)
Second Neoclassical (*defined*), 145–146
Second Renaissance Revival (*defined*), 145–146
Shaw, Richard Norman (British architect, designer of Scotland Yard Building), 125–26
Shawyer House, Charles I., 193
Shepley, Rutan & Coolidge (designers of the Warder Public Library and the Bushnell Building), 131
Shingle style (*defined*), 137
Shirtwaist style (*defined*), 147, 150
Short, Peyton (pioneer surveyor), 14
Sigma Kappa sorority house, 150
Sloan, Samuel (mid-nineteenth-century Philadelphia-based architect), 85, 122
Society of Dilettanti (organization of art-minded Englishmen), 32
South Charleston Log House, 10, 12
South Charleston Train Depot, 118-119
Springfield Builders' Supply Co., 68
Springfield Centennial Committee, 6
Springfield Country Club, 178
Springfield Engraving Company, 187
Springfield Illustrated, 121
Springview Sanitarium, 188
Star Cottage, 34, 35, 40, 42
Steamboat Gothic (*defined*), 73
Stickley, Gustav (Chicago furniture maker), 184
Stick style (*defined*), 118

St. John Sewing Machine Co, 83
St. Luke's church (near Smithfield, Virginia), 27
Stockbroker Tudor (*defined*), 183
Stroud, Rev. Charles, 92
Strozzi and Riccardi palaces, 68, 69
Stuart & Revett (scholars and authors), 32, 37
Sullivan, Louis Henri (American "form follows function" architect), **157–159**, 160, 164, 166
Sun House, Gus, 150-151
Symmes, John Cleve (early land developer and Northwest Territory judge), 14

Thomas, John H., 92
Thomas House, John H., 58
Thomas mansion, W.S., 133, 140
Thompson House, Christopher, 68
Thompson, Sir Benjamin, Count Rumford (Anglo-American inventor and physicist), 21
Thorpe (farm) home, Robert (Harmony Township), 68
Thrasher House, 11
Tittle Apartments, 151
Tocqueville, Alexis de (author of Democracy in America), 35
Tolan, T. J. (Ft. Wayne architect), 122
Transportation Building (of the 1893 Columbian Exposition in Chicago), 159
Treatise on Domestic Economy (by Catherine E. Beecher), 43
Treatise on the Theory and Practice of Landscape Gardening, A (by A. J. Downing), 51
Trinity Church (Boston), 131
Tudor Gothic Villa (*defined*), 54
Tudor label, 56, 58
Tudor style (*defined*), 181, 183
Tuileries Palace (Paris, France), 96
Tuscan style (*defined*), 77
20th Century History of Springfield and Clark County (by William Rockel), 139

Unity Temple (Chicago, Frank Lloyd Wright), 166
University of Salamanca (Spain), 191
Upjohn, Richard (nineteenth-century immigrant English architect), 67, 68, 69, 70, 77
U.S. Capitol Building, 30

Vanderbilts, the (prominent American family), 145
Vaux, Calvert (immigrant English architect), 53, 54, 67
Vendramini Palace (Venice, Italy), 69
Venetian Gothic style (partially defined), 128
Villa d'Este (Tivoli, Italy), 194
Village Builder and Supplement (by A. J. Bicknell), 103
Virginia style (*defined*), 19, 21

Walpole, Horace (son of Prime Minister Sir Robert Walpole and owner of "Strawberry Hill"), 48-49
Walter, Thomas U. (American architect, fourth architect of the U.S. Capitol) 37

Warder House, Benjamin H., 103, 131
Warder, Jeremiah (Springfield settler, early land entrepreneur), 6, 140
Warder, William (former part-owner of Warder & Barnett Flour Mills), 100, 140
Weaver House, C.I., 187
Weigand House, G., 119
Weimer House, 90
Weldon House, 37
Westcott automobile, 167
Westcott, Burton J. (founder of the Westcott Motor Co. and, along with wife Orpha, commissioned a house designed by Frank Lloyd Wright), 161, 164, 166, 167
Westcott House, 161, 164, 165
Wharton, Thomas (British gentleman and amateur artist), 6
Wheeler, Gervase (English émigré architect), 67, 114
White, Stanford (American architect), 145
Whiteley, Fassler & Kelly, 108
Whiteman, Gen. Benjamin (early settler), 14
Widow's Walk, 72
Winckleman, Johann (author), 32, 37
Winters House, John P., 83, 90
Wittenberg College, 154
Woods-Algier Funeral Home, 90
Wren Home, Edward, 133
Wright, Frank Lloyd (American architect), 56, 114, 153, 157, **159–167**, 181, 183
Wright style, Frank Lloyd (defined), 160, 165, 166

Yellow Brick style (*defined*), 174

Zimmerman Buildings, 147

George H. Berkhofer was born in New York City in 1939, but was raised in Illinois. He attended the University of Michigan and then did his graduate work at the University of Illinois. He came to Springfield, Ohio in 1966 to teach at Wittenberg University.

In 1970 he became executive director and curator of the Clark County Historical Society, where he did extensive writing and historical preservation work over the next twelve years. He directed the restoration of two historic properties.

In 1979 he helped in founding the Heritage Commission Corporation in South Charleston. He has been executive director and president of the group ever since. In this capacity he has led the local history movement in the town and again directed the preservation of three properties: The Town Hall Opera House, the 1878 Village Depot, and the 1820s log house.

Mr. Berkhofer has received awards for his preservation work from the Springfield Preservation Alliance, The National Daughters of the American Revolution, The South Charleston Heritage Commission, and the South Charleston Community Club. He is married to Karen Ipsen of Denver, Colorado and they have three children.